Praise for *Diabetic's Journey*

It gives me great pleasure to endorse *Diabetic's Journey: How Type 2 Diabetes Can Be Reversed and Cured*, written by Ernest Quansah. As a professor who specializes in this field, I was delighted to read this compelling autobiographical account of a determined individual who successfully self-cured his diabetes. The number of cases of diabetes mellitus has been increasing at an alarming rate across the globe and this unique and informative book is greatly needed.

Soon, every household will have a member suffering from type 2 diabetes. *Diabetic's Journey* will bring about greater awareness of the condition and bring to light the fact that sufferers can reverse it through natural, non-medical means.

As a senior diabetologist with more than 36 years of experience, I am really impressed with how the author shares his knowledge with others in a practical and lucid way. People will easily relate to his journey since it is written with great sincerity by a former sufferer of the condition.

Regarding the million dollar question of whether type 2 diabetes can be cured or reversed, my answer is yes. As an experienced diabetologist, I acknowledge that diabetes can be cured. If people are made aware of the causes of diabetes, and if they remove those causes, then diabetes can be reversed.

The author rightly points out that type 2 diabetes is mainly caused by lack of awareness of what one should and should not eat, plus a lack of exercise. He also rightly points out that one should never allow the diabetes to rule the body; rather, one must rule the diabetes. Definitely DIET AND EXERCISE will keep away diabetes, and as in Ernest's case, bring about a cure. Ernest explains these facts with clear reason and proof.

I have immense appreciation for this wonderful, inspiring book, which will benefit type 2 diabetics and those wanting to learn about the condition. His main message—to modify lifestyle rather than depend on drugs—will certainly have a great impact.

I thank Ernest for his great contribution to society.

                        Prof. S.M. Rajendran, M.D., FRCP(GLAS), D.Sc.
                        Professor of Diabetology and Medicine
                        Chennai Medical College Hospital

DIABETIC'S JOURNEY

DIABETIC'S JOURNEY

HOW TYPE 2 DIABETES CAN BE REVERSED AND CURED

ERNEST QUANSAH

Diabetic's Journey: How Type 2 Can Be Reversed and Cured
by Ernest Quansah

Copyright © 2017 by Ernest Quansah

All rights reserved. No part of this book may be reproduced or utilized in any form or by any means, electronic or mechanical, including photocopying or recording, or by any information storage and retrieval system, without written permission from the publisher.

This book is not written to provide medical advice, diagnosis, or treatment.

ISBN- 978-0-9947670-4-2

Published by Ernest Quansah
Website: https://diabeticsjourney.com

Printed and bound in the USA

Cover design by Ernest Quansah
Book Design by Sun Editting & Book Design (www.suneditwrite.com)

Contents

Acknowledgements 9

Introduction 11

When Bad Things Happen for Good Reasons 13

Managing Type 2 Diabetes 27

Why Do We Do Things that Hurt Us? 43

Information Is Power 51

Research on Reversing Type 2 Diabetes 67

Diabetes Healing Plan 93

Questions and Answers 113

How Type 2 Diabetes Can Be Reversed and Cured 129

About the Author 143

Other Books by Ernest Quansah 145

Acknowledgements

First and foremost, I would like to thank God for making me a type 2 diabetic, due to which I developed a desire to find a cure for the condition and which led me to take on the role of a diabetes researcher.

I want to thank Bruce McLean for recommending that I see his pharmacist-friend who was working at Sunset Pharmacy and is an expert in diabetes. To get me started, the pharmacist put me on the right vitamins and told me that type 2 diabetes could be cured. I needed to hear that.

My heartfelt gratitude also goes to my family doctor, Dr. Anthony Robinson. I thank him for diagnosing the diabetes before it took my life and for indicating what I needed to do to reverse and even cure it.

My sincere thanks also goes to Dr. Xiao Qin, who started me off on acupuncture treatments and advised me about diet and what exercise to do in order to see results in the fight against type 2 diabetes. She and Dr. Robinson truly got me started on the right path. All the individuals I have acknowledged played a part in assisting me to achieve optimum health. I could not have done it without them.

Lastly, I would like to thank three organizations: firstly, *WebMD Diabetes* for featuring how I reversed and cured my diabetes in their *WebMD Diabetes,* fall 2016 issue, page 19, as well as on their website; secondly, the International Diabetes Federation (IDF,) whose mission it is to promote diabetes care and its cure worldwide; and finally, Clyto Access, for inviting me to present my diabetes research at the International Diabetes and Degenerative Disease Conference. It was a great honour, indeed.

Introduction

It is estimated that 11% percent of Americans are diabetic and 30% are pre-diabetic. In Canada, 9% of the population is diabetic. Worldwide, there are 425 million diabetics, and experts predict that by the year 2040, if the current trend continues, one out of every eight people will be diabetic, totaling a staggering 1.8 billion diabetics worldwide. (This statistic is based on the assumption that by 2040, the world population will have reached eight billion.) Type 2 diabetes occurs within every race and culture and in any part of the world. Unlike developing nations where many are not educated about diabetes until it is too late, those of us in developed nations are more aware of diabetes and its effects. Despite this fact, far too many of us fail to act until our health has been seriously compromised. This is because type 2 diabetes, although very damaging to internal organs, is not in itself painful. As a result, it is easy for diabetics to overlook the condition and continue on the same path that brought it on.

Can type 2 diabetes be reversed and permanently cured? The International Diabetes Federation's mission statement says it can. So does the latest research, which I will talk more about in this book.

Aside from these facts, great inspiration came to me when I learned about Dr. Paula Baillie-Hamilton, PhD. After giving birth, she was not able to lose the extra weight she had gained. She then headed a research program that revealed a main cause of what had prevented her and postnatal woman in general from losing weight. This information applies to all overweight individuals. The outcome of her research led her to author *Toxic Overload*, a book especially intended to help postnatal mothers lose weight.

Inspired by Dr. Baillie-Hamilton's approach described in her book, I undertook my own research in an effort to find a way to reverse my diabetes. I used myself as the test subject, mainly because my own case was severe and if the research were to yield positive results, it would prove that even an extreme case of diabetes could be reversed.

I love what I have accomplished, but what I love most is sharing my knowledge with others and helping them reverse their type 2 diabetes.

If you have type 2 diabetes, don't just become a statistic.
Now is the time to cure it.

—Ernest Quansah

When Bad Things Happen for Good Reasons

THERE IS OVERWHELMING and mounting evidence that type 2 diabetes cannot just be reversed, but it can be cured. Such evidence was published in the *WebMD Diabetes*, fall 2016 issue, as well as on their website. Additionally, an article published in *The National Post* on March 16, 2017 brought to light research that has shown type 2 diabetes can be reversed in as little as four months.

The day my own doctor told me that my type 2 diabetes could be cured—yes, he used the word "cured"—I couldn't have been happier. What later brought me even greater happiness was when I informed him I had succeeded in reversing my diabetes and wanted to put the information into a book to help other diabetics worldwide, and he replied, "That is an excellent idea."

What Makes Me Happy

Caring about people and doing nice things for them is what makes me happy. When I was in college, the teacher in one of my classes asked the students to write what made them happy on a piece of paper and to pass their pieces of papers to the student in front of them to read. The students were surprised when they heard my answer, which was simply, "To care for and do nice things for people." Many asked, "Who wrote that answer?"

Separately, in Philosophy class, the professor asked a similar question to which I gave the same response. The professor told the class that if Ernest finds happiness in caring for people and doing nice things for them, his actions are based on selfishness, because the actions make *him* happy. (I'll let you be the judges of his opinion.)

In Peer Counselling class, the lead psychologist raised a similar question. I recounted what the philosophy professor had said about me, but in this case, the lead psychologist told me that if I stopped doing nice things for people and caring about them, I would be changing who I was.

Because of my life's objective to care about people and do nice things for them, I have often suffered greatly. I have questioned whether this approach toward others has been worth it. The remaining sections of this chapter document the challenges I have faced in my resolve to help others.

The Journey

As I sit here in front of the computer attempting to put my thoughts into words for the world to read, I wonder where to start. I am excited about what I am about to disseminate. I have heard great thinkers, like Oprah, make statements, such as: Find out what you are put on earth for and follow that path. Another remark that is tattooed in my brain was made to me by a wise man when my employment was not serving me. He said, "Sometimes the universe allows others to do terrible things to a person in order to redirect his or her destiny." It is not uncommon for unsavory things—including violent acts—to happen to people that lead them to take on a powerful role, which ends up making a difference and inspiring millions of people.

Let's take the example of Malala Yousafzai. A member of the Taliban gunned her down, but she survived. After recovering, within four years, she had gained much more influence than those who had wanted to take her life. Her quotes make people think. She has authored a book, been awarded honorary Canadian citizenship, and won the Nobel Peace Prize. Had the Taliban not made the attempt on her life, I wonder if she could have attained her current status in the world.

Sometimes people plan to destroy another. What these heartless people don't know is that their actions can play a main role in causing their victims to manifest their destiny.

My destiny has followed a similar path. It never occurred to me that, one day in my life, I would research type 2 diabetes. I aspired to become a world renowned chef, a wish that began when I was in cooking school and applied for training under the world's only high-caliber chef to be awarded a double 3-star Michelin rating. His name was Alain Ducasse. At that time, more than a decade before I was diagnosed with type 2 diabetes, the idea I might become diabetic never occurred, but I did have one most interesting thought. I don't know where the thought originated from but it just popped up in my mind. As I sat pondering in my old, blue rattan chair one evening, this thought came to me. *I would love to find a cure for a disease.* This was followed by a thought that I said aloud, "But I don't have a background in medicine." *Even if I were able to find a cure for a disease, could I achieve this without first becoming afflicted with it?* I recall this chain of thoughts as if it happened yesterday. It was the day the famed singer, Michael Jackson, died.

I had been fired from my dream job—which I loved—as Director of Food and Beverage in a good establishment for seniors. I had sacrificed everything for that company and the owner had even promised to move me to the United States to become Corporate Director of Food and Beverage with a six-figure income. That fated day, as I drove home, I began to cry while listening to my favorite jazz station. So exactly how did I lose my job?

I was diagnosed with type 2 diabetes after I was fired from this job. But let's backtrack. While working at that job, things were great—at first. As Director of Food and Beverage and having been directly interviewed and hired by the company owner, my rank was equal to that of the general manager. (The owner, who was also the CEO of the company, was the only one who could terminate my employment.) My problems first took root when the CEO would visit from the US, stop by the facility, and often refer to me as the most important person in the building. The reason he did this was mainly because, for the residents in the retirement facility, it was all about food and camaraderie. (These elderly residents looked forward to the food so much that on Sundays, they would wear their best cloths for dinner and invite family members.) I was exceptionally good at creating the type of environment that the elderly residents very much appreciated. I come from a culture where the elderly are given immense value and are cherished for their storytelling and life experience, which they pass on to their offspring.

The CEO would call me "Bro." He would say that if I was visiting the US and in Arizona area, I should call him and come and stay at his mansion. According to the general manager, when other managers had concerns, the CEO would not fly out of the United States to go and see them, as he did in my case. The general manager once commented that this must mean that the CEO must really like me. To make matters worse, I once told the general manager, Mr. David Walters, that I wanted to be a GM one day. According to Mr. Walters, when he himself was hired by the company, he was told that he would be made Director of Operations. That position had eluded him, as it was passed on to a young man who had married the CEO's daughter. There is more background to Mr. Walters's mounting discontent and envy of me—Mr. Walters's partner had recently left him for another man. He would sometimes come to work and cry.

The sequence of events leading to the loss of my job goes like this: A woman (we will call Angie) once came looking for work at the facility. She said that her husband had died of cancer. She had children and worked in a fast food restaurant but wanted a better job. I offered her work out of compassion. A week into Angie's employment, Mr. Walters asked me to fire her. I explained to him that Angie was a single mom whose husband had died of cancer, so we should have compassion on her and give her a chance. Mr. Walters explained that he was not running a charity and that Angie had rough edges. Angie was not very educated. Among those on my staff, one had a degree in psychology. She and others could not accept that Angie was their supervisor. They would threaten to quit their jobs. To make matters worse, any time Angie had the chance, she would go on Facebook while the staff she was in charge of worked. Angie would also pick fights with the other female staff members. One of them was a highly-skilled Greek woman who had owned a restaurant at one time. She was excellent at her job. Angie once fought with her until the woman broke into tears. At other times, Angie would say things like, "Greek people are loud and obnoxious" or "I should fire the Greek lady."

I ultimately decided to terminate Angie's employment. Somehow, she got wind of my intentions. So, I had on my hands a staff member whose work I was about to terminate and a general manager who felt lied to about being promoted by the CEO (in addition to his partner having left him,) all this on top of the fact that the CEO would tell the managers that I was the most important person in the building. Now, these two (Mr. Walters and Angie) formulated a plan to get my job terminated and put it into action. Angie told Mr. Walters that staff members had approached her saying that I was a big, black guy and they were afraid of me.

One Monday morning, Mr. Walters approached me and told me that he wanted to talk with me. He informed me that accusations had been leveled against me, so I was being terminated. Later, some of the staff informed me that Angie and Mr. Walters had called them to Mr. Walters's office and promised to give them full-time hours if they would jointly file accusations of abuse against me. Because Mr. Walters had not hired me and had no power to fire me, he first sent a letter with the accusations to the company lawyer and the lawyer then contacted the CEO, who approved my termination. I was hurt that the same woman that I had twice protected from termination had turned against me. Prior to these events, on Mr. Walters's birthday, I ordered a cake and gathered all the staff and managers together to wish and sing happy birthday to him. Furthermore, every morning I would make breakfast for him and have it delivered. These thoughts took over my emotions. Since Mr. Walters had the habit of saying terrible things about the CEO and his son-in-law during management meetings, I wrote to the CEO's son-in-law telling him these things Mr. Walters had said about him and his father-in-law. I mentioned that on one occasion, Mr. Walters said to me that I tended to hire male staff and because of that, I must be gay and needed to come out of the closet, followed by him saying, "Do you want to be my bitch." This highly inappropriate and offensive language was heard by a witness. The son-in-law who had been given Mr. Walters's dream job as Director of Operations and had become Mr. Walters's boss went to Mr. Walters and fired him. Once he had fired Mr. Walters, he sent me an email letting me know that Mr. Walters's employment had been terminated.

What goes around comes around. The female staff members that had been promised more work-hours if they would team up and make accusations against me did not get what they were promised. Out of disgust, a couple of them quit their jobs and sent me an apology for what they had done. As for Angie, she brought about her own job termination. Once I was let go, she went after my job, which had been given to a chef. In an attempt to accomplish her goal, she would invite a 19-year-old male server who worked at the facility out for drinks. After the drinks, she would take him to her home. After a few weeks of this, Angie asked the 19-year-old to go to the new general manager and tell him that the new chef touched his buttocks and that the staff had witnessed the occurrence. The young man did as Angie had asked him and told the GM that the female staff had witnessed it. The female staff members were called to the GM's office. When questioned, they told the GM that they had not witnessed any touching and that Angie had come to them and asked them to say that they had witnessed the chef touching the 19-year-old server. The staff proceeded to tell the GM that Angie had done the same thing to me—created such similar accusations. Angie was called to the office but was not fired at that time. Maybe Angie went through an awakening, realizing that something was about to happen to her. The staff called me to tell me that Angie said she should not have done what she did to me. The following Monday, when Angie arrived at work, she was called to the office first thing in the morning and fired. What goes around comes around.

If my experience at the hands of Angie and Mr. Walters was not bad enough, it was about to get worse. My experience that you are about hear was a direct, personal attack. Let it be said that evil does exist and sometimes the workplace can be so toxic that it can make one sick. In my first week at this particular job, the manager told me that I needed to be careful about what I said around the female employees at work. He said, "One day they are flirting with you, but the next thing you know, they turn around and attack you because they are in a bad mood." This manager, named Mrs. Clarkson, then informed me that she was to retire in four years and would like me to commit to the job and not quit on her because all her previous cooks had quit on her. As one who always wants to please others, I agreed to her request.

Shortly after, one of the staff approached me and informed me that I should be careful because Mrs. Clarkson was an unforgiving manager. To make a long story short, Mrs. Clarkson turned out to have psychopathic tendencies. Dr. Robert D. Hare, a renowned Canadian researcher in the field of criminal psychology clearly defines the tendencies of a psychopath. His definitions helped me understand the nature of such people. In summation, I am listing some these tendencies:

- They accuse their victims of the same things they do to hurt their victims.

- They are prolific liars and even when they are caught, they insist they did nothing wrong.

- When psychopaths do something wrong and are confronted by the victim, they look for something they can use against them. When they find it, they say things like, "You said I did this and that to you but you did this and that to this person. You are no better than I am."

- They have no conscience, thus, they don't care how deeply their actions hurt and injure their victims.

- One of their patent responses when questioned about having done something wrong is to say, "I have done nothing wrong. I feel like I am being attacked."

- They know what they are doing and go so far as to plan to hurt their victims and plan how they will defend themselves when they are caught.

- If their victims forgive them, they may say things to others, such as, "Why isn't any action being taken against that person." If action is not taken against their victims, it makes them feel that they have become the victim.

- If their victims forgive them, they may say things, such as, "If I did something wrong, why isn't any action being taken against me?" In other words, if they hurt others and are forgiven, they believe they have done nothing wrong; that is why no action is being taken against them. They lie about everything, but in their minds, the lies they tell are the truth. This thought pattern makes them some of the most dangerous people in the world, according to Dr Hare.

- Psychopaths are often such good liars that they are known for lying in court and getting away with it. They are also known for lying to law enforcement officials and getting away with the wrongs they have committed.

I will not get into the details of the mistreatment I was subjected to at the hands of Mrs. Clarkson, but I will say that it was extensive. Demonstrating her psychopathic tendencies, Mrs. Clarkson denied any of the things she did to hurt me and also what she did to one of the female staff who had to take stress leave as a result of the treatment she had endured. Mrs. Clarkson lied to staff and used intimidation tactics, including threats. For example: she would say that if I were to report her mistreatment of the staff to her superiors, she would call her lawyer. In our lives, there are sometimes past experiences that we try to block out of our minds. Despite now having such an inclination, I feel my story needs to be told so that people may know what can go on in the workplace.

Bad Can Never Win Over Good

Just when I was about to file a civil lawsuit against Mrs. Clarkson for sexual harassment, I had a most amazing dream which caused me to hold off on the lawsuit. In the dream, I was walking on white sand that encircled a pond which had pure, blue water. Behind me, in the pond, was a massive cave. In front of me was more white sand that led to a hill located on the other side of the pond. I walked along the path of white sand and as I passed the cave, from within it, a huge snake about 30 inches in diameter emerged and lunged at me. The snake wanted to wrap around me but could not because it needed me to be in the pond so that it could drag me into the dark cave. Realizing its inability to succeed, it decided to retreat back into the cave. As it began to retreat, I caught a glimpse of the snakes head. Its face was the face of Mrs. Clarkson. Right at that moment, I heard a voice telling me that if I kept walking and didn't step into the pond, I would reach the top of the hill that lay on the other side.

Life's Lessons

The two work-related experiences I have just shared were necessary in pointing me to what I was put on earth to do. It is part of human nature that when things don't go exactly the way we planned, (as they rarely do,) we usually become upset. But let us not forget that the choices we make for ourselves are not always the correct ones. Sometimes, unless the universe causes us to have terrible experiences that force us to move on, (sometimes at the hands of others,) we never reach our full potential or become the person we were placed on the earth to become. If I had not encountered my challenging experiences, I would not have reached where I am now, which is to have found a cure for type 2 diabetes. The universe uses people who choose to be losers to help winners win. I won by manifesting my destiny. Here is a good analogy: For an arrow to hit the bull's-eye, it has to be first placed on the string of a bow and then drawn back before it can be released and launched towards its target. When your boss uses you, as most do, and then fires you, all he or she is doing is pulling you back and launching you (firing you) towards the target you were put on earth to reach.

Continuing on from when I was fired from work: On my way home, I began to crave sugar. I stopped by the supermarket and purchased the largest jug of lemonade I could find. I drank it for the rest of the day and the following day until it was finished. My dietary bad habits would ensue. Here are a few of them: Often, I would eat a pile of cookies for breakfast. I would also regularly buy a box of chocolates, start with eating one, pick up another later on and end up polishing off the whole box by the end of the day. Then, at night, I would drive to a 24/7 convenience store, purchase a large Slurpee and go home and sit on my balcony where I would down the whole thing. After some time of such practices, I found myself running to the bathroom every 10 to 20 minutes to urinate. My weight began to drop very rapidly and not knowing what was going on, I was happy that I was shedding the pounds. My joy over the weight loss quickly turned to panic. I noticed that, each morning, a thick, whitish substance covered my tongue and appeared in the corners of my eyes. When it began to worsen, I went to see my doctor. He asked me a few questions and ordered an immediate blood glucose test. That same day, within three hours of my first visit, his receptionist called and requested me to return to the office immediately. When I entered his office, my doctor stated, "You have become diabetic. Do you know the danger you have put yourself in? You are not far from having a cardiac arrest." His face had turned red.

The diagnosis came as a heavy blow. I could not believe it. I sat there with my face down staring at the floor. I was in shock. The test showed that I had a blood glucose level of 21.9 millimoles per litre or 394.6 milligrams, more than five times the normal levels of 4.0 to 6.5 mmol/L.

My doctor further explained the diagnosis as such: He said that the sticky whitish substance appearing on my tongue and in the corners of my eyes each morning was the buildup of sugar in my body trying to find a way to exit instead of killing me. He said I was lucky to be alive. It has now been eight years since that diagnosis and I still wonder at the fact that I survived.

A very traumatic circumstance occurred when my doctor put me on large doses of drugs because of the stage of diabetes I was in. One day, I woke up and could not see. In a state of utter panic I thought to myself: *No, I've gone blind. No way—I've gone blind.* The drugs the doctor had put me on had caused some of the sugar in my blood to withdraw from my eyes at a rapid rate and this resulted in the loss of vision by which all objects were a complete blur, (but at the time I didn't know the cause). I called a friend next door who came over and dialed my doctor's number for me. I was only able to set up an appointment for the next day. I will give the details of this story in Chapter 3, "Why Do We Do Things that Hurt Us?"

For two years, I took the traditional medications prescribed by my doctor. At the same time, I tried a wide variety of alternative cure plans. I didn't want to just give in to the condition. At the end of the two-year period, I had had no success in reversing my diabetes. One day, I collapsed onto the floor next to my bed. I couldn't handle it anymore. It was all too much. Leg amputation, eventual liver disease, heart disease, and a slew of diseases that could be triggered by type 2 were staring me in the face. As these thoughts rushed through my mind, I started crying. I felt helpless.

I understood that I had made myself a type 2 diabetic by my own lifestyle choices, such as the foods I had eaten and due to a lack of exercise. I had acquired the type of diabetes that most type 2 diabetics have—the non-hereditary type.

With my failure to overcome the diabetes, I started to take on the role of a diabetes researcher. I had done enough of blindly following the treatments plans of others. It was time for me to get as educated as possible about diabetes by doing my own research, and further, experimentation with natural treatments for bringing about a reversal. Based on my findings, I made tests on myself—an extreme case. I was not expecting too much, but since nothing else had worked, I just wanted to see if my findings and experimentation would yield any results. Ultimately, I developed a formula that bore significant results.

My doctor, Dr. Anthony Robinson, was astonished when he saw the results of my blood test taken after I felt I had made significant progress in my reversal experimentation. As he looked at the results, I recalled that when he first diagnosed me, his face turned red. This time, as he reviewed my test results, his face lit up. "Congratulations! You are no longer a diabetic. Tell me," he asked in amazement, "How did you do it?" This was February 21st, 2012. He was sincerely astonished that I had reversed my diabetes. He had assumed that I was resigned to taking drugs while waiting for the diabetes to progress to the type 1, the irreversible type. He told the other doctors and the front staff as we walked to the front of the office, "Congratulate this man. He has cured his diabetes." Before I left, he printed a copy of the lab report and told me, "Here, take this and flaunt it. Show it to everyone. Show it to your pharmacist. Tell everyone." When I left his office that day, I was so overjoyed that I accidently drove through a red light.

Even at this very moment—March 14th, 2017—as I chronicle this experience, the fact that my diabetes is gone, and thinking of all I underwent—it seems like a dream. It still has not fully registered. My doctor used these words to describe me, "You are very unique." I knew what he was saying. I also knew what he meant when he asked me how I had done it. I had achieved something he had never suspected that I would. He told me that in his forty years of practicing medicine, I was only his second patient who decided to reverse my diabetes and followed through with the efforts.

Managing Type 2 Diabetes

I THOUGHT I UNDERSTOOD the ways of the world. It is true. Money makes people do bad things to other human beings. When I was diagnosed with the type 2 diabetes, I knew little of the world that surrounded the condition. As I continued along my personal journey, the tentacles of this world caught me and pulled me into it. These tentacles were greed, lies, taking advantage of others when they are vulnerable, and the preventing of diabetics from understanding and gaining knowledge about their eventual demise. I came to understood that all this was being done so that unwitting victims could be harnessed for maximum profit. During my research and attempts to heal myself, I discovered that there were individuals, so-called "top" diabetes bloggers, and hundreds upon hundreds of companies, (perhaps even thousands,) all bent on profiting from vulnerable diabetics.

They do this by successfully promoting diabetes management to 90% percent of type 2 diabetics. There is money to be made by misleading diabetics.

For two years, I had tried to simply manage (not try to reverse or cure) my diabetes, as most diabetics are led to do. The ads of the companies promoting diabetes management through their drugs and treatments have done a great job in convincing diabetics to believe their intentionally misleading information. I understand that the pancreas no longer works and the patient requires manual injections of insulin when one has type 1 diabetes, but in the case of type 2 diabetes, the condition is mostly acquired through lifestyle choices. This also applies to obesity. So how did we arrive at just managing type 2 diabetes?

We live in a society that believes technology and science are always right, and also, we must take the word of people in positions of authority in these fields. These so-called authorities have convinced diabetics to settle with *managing* type 2 diabetes by using pharmaceutical drugs.

I maintain that the global society is not as caring as we might think. Many years ago, I saw a report about how a group of people were able to convince one individual within their group to side with the rest of the group members and accept an incorrect statement as truthful fact. Let me explain how the experiment was conducted:

Twenty lines were drawn on a blackboard in a classroom of 20 students. The professor conducting the experiment asked 19 of the students to form one group. He then instructed the 19 students that they were part of an experiment to show how easy it is for the majority to influence the minority. The 19 that formed the group were then taken aside and instructed that during class, they would be asked to count the 20 lines that the professor put on the blackboard, but say that they only counted 19 lines. The smartest student in that class, the 20th student, was not informed of the experiment.

Later, all the 20 students were asked to count the lines on the board, as planned. The 19 students who were privy to the experiment said they counted only 19 lines. The smartest student—the 20th student—counted the lines and said he counted 20 lines. In fact, he insisted: "There are 20 lines on the board. Not 19." The rest of the class disagreed with him. This disagreement went back and forth for a while as each party wanted to win the debate. The scientist asked the single student, "How is it that 19 students counted 19 lines and yet you, a single student, have counted 20 lines?" The master of the class, the professor, instructed the single student to carefully recount the lines. Just as he was instructed, the student fulfilled the instructions. "Oh, I see," he admitted. "They are right. There are 19 lines."

Of course, he was correct at first when he asserted that there were 20 lines on the board, but because all of the other students, as well as the professor, insisted that there were only 19 lines, the smartest student in that class became convinced that he was wrong and sided with the 19 classmates who were, in fact, the ones who were wrong. With persistence, the experimenter convinced the smart student to align his mind with the rest of the class.

Like the smart student who was convinced that he was not smart enough to discriminate between 19 and 20 lines, and ended up accepting that his classmates were correct and not him, type 2 diabetics believe what their doctors tell them. We believe what the TV ads tell us—"live with diabetes and manage it." In the case of type 1 diabetes, (where the pancreas no longer works,) as well as with type 2 diabetes which is inherited, these two types of diabetes are not acquired by lifestyle choices. These two categories of diabetes cannot be reversed. However, an acceptance of living with and manage diabetes, regardless of which type, has become the worldwide norm and standard. This begs the question: If all the types of diabetes must only be managed, why does the International Diabetes Federation's own mission statement clearly say that their mission is to promote diabetes care and cure worldwide? This makes one question why the American Diabetes Association and the Canadian Diabetes Association (both members of the International Diabetes Association) promote managing type 2 diabetes and not curing it. It means that these organizations are in conflict with the International Diabetes Federation's mission. I believe in the International Diabetes Federation's mission. I hope that just as the 19 students convinced one student to interpret 20 lines on a black board as 19 lines, that all type 2 diabetics who acquire their condition though lifestyle will believe in the International Diabetes Association's mission—to promote diabetes care and cure.

Type 2 diabetes can be reversed. I am convinced of this not only because of my personal success, but also because of the declarations of some of the most highly respected medical organizations and results of other researchers. All this should leave no doubt in the minds of diabetics.

In 2016, after I completed my work as a type 2 diabetes researcher, I was graciously invited by James Matkin, a Harvard Law graduate and a constitutional lawyer based in Vancouver, BC Canada, to join Academia.edu where I posted a paper which I titled *The Case Against Managing Type 2 Diabetes*. The paper has been downloaded by other Academia researchers. Here it is for you to read.

The Case Against Managing Type 2 Diabetes

Type 2 diabetes is the largest non-communicable disease in the world. According to the American Diabetes Association®, in 2012, 29.1 million Americans had diabetes. That is 9.3% of the population. Eighty-six million Americans aged 20 or over were pre-diabetic. Data from the Public Health Agency of Canada shows that in 2011, 2,359,252 Canadians were diabetic. These numbers have been on a steady increase and will continue to be so. Worldwide, in 2016, the number of diabetics was estimated at 421 million. (These are the most recent collective statistics.) In late 2011, one report suggested that by the year 2030, one out of every eight people in the world will be diabetic—a staggering figure of about 800 million people. The amount spent each year on diabetes in the United States far exceeds most nations' five-year GDP. The majority of people believe that type 2 diabetes is an incurable disease. One evening, I had friends over for dinner. After the feasting was over, I presented them with the cover design I was considering for the first edition of this book, which was soon to be released. One of the women in attendance asked, "How are you going to convince people that type 2 diabetes is not a disease and that it is a reversible condition?" For many days, I pondered the answer to the question. We live in a time where emphasis is placed on scientific facts and research. To date, there is no research that has proved that type 2 diabetes *cannot* be reversed—none. Despite this being the case, we are only told that type 2 diabetics have to manage their diabetes. There are so-called experts—including medical doctors—who claim that no one knows exactly what goes on inside the body of a diabetic and that type 2 diabetes is *not* caused by the accumulation of sugar, causing the body to become insulin resistant. The problem I have with their argument is that if no one knows what goes on inside the diabetic's body, why is it that one of the latest type 2 diabetes drug ads states that the drug prevents some of the sugar ingested from reaching the kidneys, thus lowering blood sugar?

Symptoms of the onset of type 2 diabetes

I was diagnosed with type 2 diabetes at the age of 46. Prior to the diagnosis, I experienced these symptoms:

- Feeling thirsty followed by a strong craving for sugary drinks or sweets

- Frequent trips to the bathroom to urinate

- Frequent trips to the toilet, as food did not stay in the stomach

- Rapid weight loss of about 10 pounds each month

- A very large boil at the base of my head

- Small, but several boils on my genitals.

These symptoms were followed by the appearance of a white sticky substance on my tongue, as well as in the corner of my eyes each morning when I awoke. In a panic, I ultimately made a trip to the doctor's office. My doctor informed me that I was very close to going into cardiac arrest and that the whitish substance covering my tongue and in the corner of the eyes was sugar trying to exit my body so that it would not kill me.

My blood glucose test showed my blood sugar level to be 21.8. The highest level in Canada recorded is 30 millimoles, the level where the onset of a coma is possible. (In the US, blood glucose meters stop at 600 milligrams, which is equivalent to about 33 millimoles. That meant that the level of sugar in my blood was 396.76 milligrams! I have been told that I was lucky I did not die.

What is managing type 2 diabetes?

Managing type 2 diabetes is a process whereby the patient is prescribed pharmaceutical drugs for their diabetes. The patient is required to take a certain dosage prior to or with meals. The dosage amount is dependent upon test results. A diabetic's doctor orders quarterly blood glucose tests. After diagnosis, I did what medical doctors and the TV ads said diabetics should do—managed the diabetes. Later, I would take a critical step, which was to search for a diabetes cure. Upon a visit to my physician, I asked him open-ended questions, such as: "Dr. Robinson, can type 2 diabetes be cured?" His response to this particular question was "Yes." I then understood that I had to research a cure and in the process discovered literature upon literature stating that type 2 diabetes is not a disease, but a reversible condition—like obesity—that can be permanently cured.

Prior to asking my doctor if diabetes could be cured, I was managing it like millions of other diabetics. As I've already said, both type 2 diabetics and non-diabetics—as well as most medical doctors—see diabetes as a disease that should be managed. This is not correct. Every informed medical doctor will attest to this.

Managing diabetes meant I would remain a diabetic. At the clinic I was sent to for treatment, I was informed how to manage the diabetes and told that type 2 diabetes is progressive and that my type 2 diabetes would eventually reach the point where the pancreas would die and therefore not be able to secrete insulin. As well, it could cause the following catastrophic ailments:

- heart disease
- liver failure
- blindness
- leg amputation
- diabetic ulcers
- blindness
- impotence.

The more I evaluated my condition and the above diseases, the more irrelevant and pointless managing appeared, thus, I found myself forced to either research a cure with the help of experts, or allow my health to be overtaken by one or more of the above.

Is type 2 diabetes a disease?

The term "disease" has two definitions.

1. By definition, cancerous tumors, Ebola, herpes, heart disease, etc. are diseases, even when less than one thousand people are identified with such an ailment. These are serious diseases.

2. When only a few people in the world were obese—for example—the condition was not considered a disease. However, as more people became obese, institutions, such as the pharmaceutical drug developers were the first to refer to the increase in weight gain as the disease of obesity. Type 2 diabetes shares a similarity with this example. As more people acquired what many doctors

saw as the condition of type 2 diabetes, the pharmaceutical intuitions quickly termed the increase as the spread of a "disease." Thus, a condition—which is not a disease but an increase in the number of people with a condition—is soon termed a disease.

Once a condition—such as type 2 diabetes—comes to be termed a disease, the institutions that made the declaration then get down to creating a drug for the so-called disease. This means, rather than establishing the cause of a condition and providing the information to people about how to prevent or reverse it, the condition/disease is allowed to continue and the drugs are sold to mask the symptoms. The fact is that the symptoms are there to tell you to make simple lifestyle improvements. The drugs should only be used when one has not been successful in reversing their condition by natural means.

In respect to drugs manufactured for type 2 diabetes, the function of such drugs is to allow the diabetic to continue to consume refined sugar. Yet, it is the refined sugar that is the main cause of type 2 diabetes in the first place (along with overeating of foods high in sugar). Therefore, the drug defeats the purpose for which it was developed. How so? The sole purpose of the drug is to make it possible for the diabetic to continue to consume refined sugar and if refined sugar is the main cause of type 2 diabetes, then this means that the drug *keeps* the diabetic a diabetic.

There is absolutely nothing good or positive about managing a condition that can be cured: this fact is supported by many medical doctors. One must consider that by only *managing* diabetes with drugs, this can lead to stroke and various other diseases. If you are a type 2 diabetic, should you manage the diabetes while waiting for outcomes such as blindness or leg amputation and a shortened lifespan? No caring person would wish this fate on any living creature, so why would you create this for yourself when it is possible to get your full health back after being diagnosed with this reversible condition?

Understanding type 2 diabetes

Type 2 diabetes, or diabetes mellitus, occurs when a person's body becomes insulin resistant. A normally functioning body is insulin sensitive.

Insulin resistance

Insulin resistance is the physical condition in which the body ceases to respond to insulin, a secretion produced by the pancreas whose main purpose is to transport sugars inside the body to the cells within the muscles and the blood stream to be used as energy. Insulin resistance occurs when there is an insufficient amount of insulin secreted by the pancreas for the transport of excess sugars in the body, which have been acquired through food consumption. From a young age, one consumes processed foods, sugary drinks, and so forth, and once one reaches the age of forty or over, there is a heavy buildup of sugar in the body and the insulin generated lacks the capacity to transport the excess sugar to the muscles for use as energy. The excess sugar settles in the body, particularly in the muscles. This is the main reason why type 2 diabetics are known for their lack of energy. Lack of energy also means lack of physical strength. When the body becomes insulin resistant, that individual is diagnosed and termed a diabetic.

Insulin sensitivity

Insulin sensitivity is the physical condition in which the body is able to utilize sugars for energy. Utilization of sugars for energy occurs when insulin produced by the pancreas—a small organ located below the stomach—transports sugar to the muscle cells where it used as energy. A body that is insulin sensitive is a diabetes-free body; which means, it is functioning the way a non-diabetic body should function. The characteristics of a healthily functioning, non-diabetic body are these:

- A healthy liver
- Clear, normal eyesight
- A non-diseased heart
- Properly functioning internal organs
- Proper levels of probiotics in the intestinal walls
- Prevention of leg amputation
- Prevention of diabetic ulcers.

The opposite of insulin sensitivity is insulin resistance.

The cost of managing diabetes

A couple of factors should be considered before a type 2 diabetic resigns himself/herself to diabetes management. Equally, government health departments should consider these factors in their approach to the condition. Research on diabetes is focused on managing the condition and developing even more drugs for this purpose. What needs to be done is for unbiased, independent bodies with no personal interest in manufacturing drugs to exert all efforts to find a cure. Until then, you, the diabetic should determine if type 2 diabetes can indeed be reversed and cured, as indicated by Dr. Anthony Robinson and myself, and other experts who have researched and confirmed the assertion of many doctors—that type 2 diabetes can be cured. By believing that type 2 diabetes is a non-curable disease, victims are easily encouraged to choose the option of managing their diabetes. The American Diabetes Association released statistics on March 6, 2013 estimating that the total cost of diabetes in the United States rose to $245 billion in 2012 from $174 billion in 2007. The sum of $245 billion included $176 billion in direct medical costs and $69 billion in reduced productivity. Read more about this at: http://www.diabetes.org/advocacy/news-events/cost-of-diabetes.html?referrer=https://www.google.ca/#sthash.j7490exx.dpuf

The above figures reflect what the United States alone spends on diabetes each year. Once we begin to take into consideration the number of people worldwide afflicted with diabetes, the amount spent yearly is staggering. Separately, further data from the ADA shows that the average diabetic has a medical expenditure of about **$7,900** each year. Curing type 2 diabetes means less money exhausted by a country and its people.

I extend an invitation to all nations and their governments to review whether or not it is sensible and financially feasible to continue spending on managing diabetes while ignoring to look into the cure.

Ernest Quansah, independent diabetes researcher, consultant, educator, and author.
Visit: https://diabetesselfcure.com/

End of the Academia article

The Challenge: One of my favorite philosophers, who was also a scientist, mathematician, and astronomer, was an Arab-Muslim man born in Basra c. 965 named Ibn al-Haytham. He is also known as Alhazen. As an educator, to prevent error during decision-making, Alhazen devised a method for drawing a conclusion, which he taught his students. This method is now widely used in courts of law. Thus, in courts of law, judges do not make their final decision or ruling based on hearsay. They make the decision based on the evidence presented.

There is no evidence supporting the notion that type 2 diabetes cannot be reversed or even cured. In a court of law, judges throw out hearsay. If there is no evidence that type 2 diabetes cannot be reversed, then the idea of living with and managing diabetes should be thrown out of the diabetic's mind.

***

A major eye-opener during my journey was learning how consumers are lied to and misled. The deception is relentless and unyielding. Those doing the misleading want the consumers' money at all costs. But all things have their opposites. I have also encountered people who, at any cost, are honest in their dealings with other human beings. My awareness of this began with a Latter-Day-Saint man that I met. During a conversation with him, he informed me that when he went into business, others in the same industry approached him and told him that if he would be dishonest, he would make ten times the profit. He said to me that despite the advice he was given, he resolved to be completely honest in his business practices. With this policy of honesty, he was successful, sent all his children to medical school and even bought his own plane. It was his words of wisdom that opened my eyes to see how business is often conducted in the world. People with the trait of honesty in the medical field did assure me that my condition could be reversed. For example, when I went to a Traditional Chinese Medicine college, I was encouraged by Dr. Xiao Chen, a practitioner with 25 years of experience in traditional Chinese medicine and 10 years in western medicine. Other such positive influences included the doctor of naturopathic medicine that I saw, a pharmacist who specializes in working with diabetics, and lastly, my dermatologist, Dr. Allan. I went to see Dr. Allan in November of 2012. He asked me how I was. I told him how I had revered my type 2 diabetes and that it took me just 21 days, once I had found the right formula. He responded, "If people would eat moderately and exercise regularly, 90% of their ailments would disappear, including heart conditions and diabetes."

What does *disappear* mean? Gone forever. Cured.

Dr. Allan continued: "But people don't want to listen. They put their faith in so-called modern science. For every little thing they ask, 'Isn't there a drug for this? Isn't there a drug for that?'"

These people I just mentioned—who were my positive influences—are experienced in their fields of practice. Those who say that type 2 diabetes can only be managed include inexperienced doctors and doctors who have been bought off and influenced to withhold the truth about a cure. This type of doctor tells diabetic patients that the condition cannot be reversed and that they need to manage it. Nurses also teach what they have been taught: that type 2 diabetes can only be managed. I sympathize with diabetics, since many doctors, as well as nurses have been misled, and therefore, misinform diabetes patients.

My hearts truly goes out to the hundreds and millions of diabetics who feel as though they have no other option but to live with their condition. Living with and managing type 2 diabetes acquired through lifestyle choices is distressing because at some point, it will likely progress to type 1 diabetes and eventually take the person's life, but not before the diabetes induces several serious diseases that I have already mentioned.

My journey has been worth the struggle. It has been very educational.

Keep up with the Facts

I recall that when I was in elementary school several decades ago, we learned that there were nine planets and one sun in our planetary system. For me and the other students, it seemed that this was the constitution of the entire universe. Fast-forward to the mid 1990s and we learned from astronomers that there were an estimated 200 billion galaxies making up our universe.

With increased power of the tools for research, astronomers have come up with a new estimation of the number of galaxies in the observable universe. NASA published a report on October 13, 2016, which stated that by means of surveys taken by NASA's Hubble Space Telescope and other observatories, astronomers have calculated that there are approximately 10 times more galaxies in the universe than the estimate of 200 billion made in the mid 1990s.

The point I would like to make here is that we can draw a parallel between the changing view of the universe and current research on type 2 diabetes. Some years ago, it was believed that this diabetic condition could only be managed (not reversed or cured) through the use of pharmaceutical drugs. It is now 2017 and articles written by physicians and diabetes researchers can be found in publications such as *Readers Digest* and on the WebMD website in which recognized experts reveal research that has shown that type 2 diabetes can be reversed and cured. As one who almost lost my life to diabetes, I feel that diabetics are being done an injustice when they are advised to simply manage their condition when there is evidence to support the possibility of reversal and cure.

In this modern world of science, research, and technological advancement, how is the idea that type 2 diabetes can only be managed any different from one saying that there are only 200 million galaxies in the universe or even that the world is flat? How is an outdated view not denial of what is fact and true?

Why Do We Do Things That Hurt Us?

WHEN I WAS diagnosed, I repented over the decisions I had made that hurt me. When I was a child, my grandparents owned and operated the largest bakery in the town where we lived in Ghana. Flour, butter, and sugar were delivered to their warehouse by the truckload. I had easy access to sugar and made use of it. Many days, I would make sugar water, then dip freshly baked bread into it and eat it. Afterward, I would drink the rest of the sugar water. I did this day in and day out. For years, I regularly consumed sugar, soft drinks, chocolate, candy bars, and all sorts of sweets.

In my adulthood, when I bought a box of chocolates, I would eat one, and then before bed, I would eat another one. I would tell myself that since I had eaten some of the chocolate, I needed to even it out by eating half the box. In the middle of the night, if I woke up, I would go directly to the kitchen cupboards for more of the chocolate. I would take one piece. Then I'd go back to my bedroom and say to myself, "Maybe just one more." The next thing I knew, the box of chocolates would be empty. I also had no problem eating cookies first thing in the morning before I had breakfast and as the last snack before bed. I would intentionally read before sleeping at night just so that I could bring cookies or other sweets to bed and snack on them while I read. I did not have the ability to say "no" to sweets and we all know how addicting sugar is.

As I mentioned in the opening chapter, these unhealthy eating practices worsened after I lost my job. The result was waking up each morning to find a whitish, sticky substance on my eyelids and later it began to show up on my tongue. People tell me that I am lucky to be alive because I was such an extreme case by the time I was diagnosed. But I do feel the pressure of the situation put me into the role of a diabetes researcher. Before this new role, when I worked as a chef, I was so busy that I did not take care of my health. Consumption of cookies and finishing off with a soda drink is not so uncommon. In my case, when I came home from work I would be so tired, I would eat nothing but sweets. My staff warned me about the consequences when they noticed that I was drinking a lot of soda drinks and eating cookies. Like many people do when given good advice, I ignored what said.

The image on the next page is the photocopy of the blood test that led to my being diagnosed as a type 2 diabetic.

Had I not gone to see the doctor and instead continued even a few more days drinking and eating refined sugar in the quantities I was, I would have gone into cardiac arrest. This is what my doctor informed me. If the cardiac arrest had happened at home when I was by myself, I could have died. I had put my life in danger without knowing it.

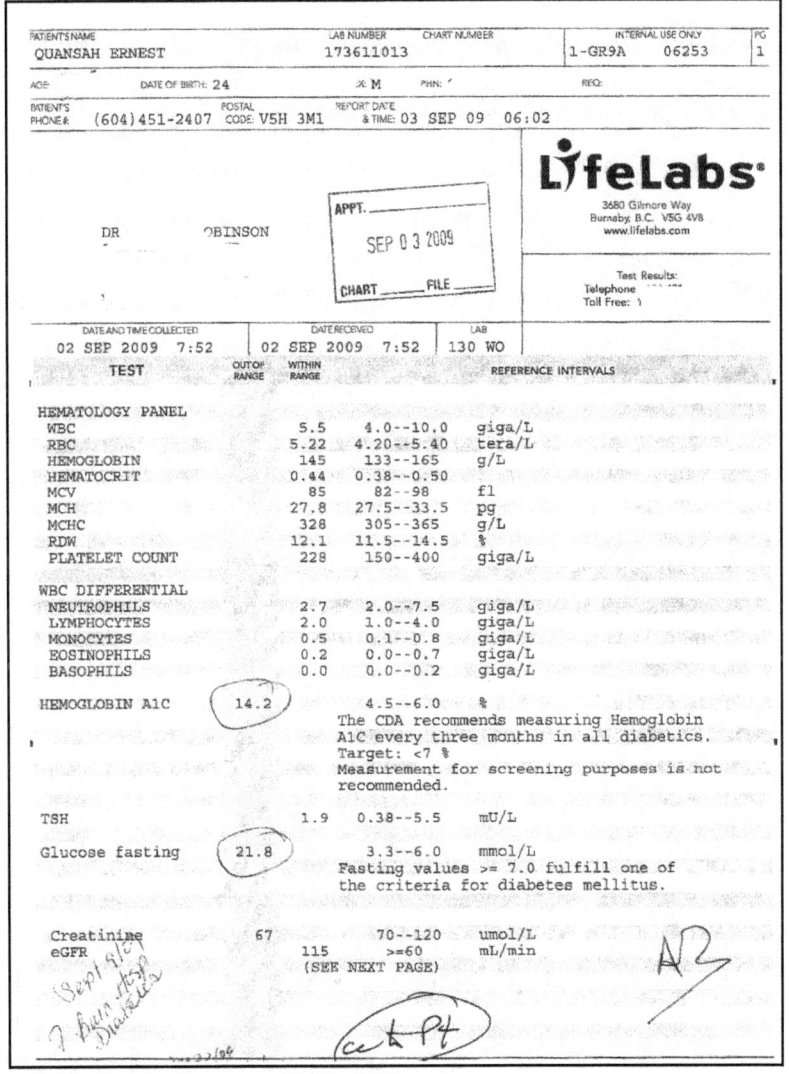

Blood test that led to my being diagnosed as a type 2 diabetic.

Details about the Day I Was Diagnosed

To some extent, I have described this day in Chapter 1. I believe it is of benefit to my readers to know the details.

Seeing the sticky whitish substance on my tongue and in my eyes each morning I was compelled to go see my doctor—this was September 2, 2009. I described to him my craving for sugar and the frequent urination that was occurring. He examined me and told me, "I suspect you have become a diabetic." He filled out a form and asked me to have a blood glucose test done. The next morning, September 3, 2009, I was in line at the nearest blood test clinic at 7AM. That same day, at 1:45 PM, I received a call. It was my doctor's receptionist. "Ernest, you need to come back to see Dr. Robinson. It is urgent," she said. "When do you think you can get here?"

"I will leave now," I replied. Since I didn't know much about diabetes and couldn't have conceived of the diagnosis, I thought my blood test must have revealed some sort of dangerous disease. I could not drive to the doctor's office fast enough—I was highly anxious to hear what the urgent finding was.

When I arrived, the receptionist led me to an examination room. About 10 minutes later, the doctor came in. His face was red, as I have already mentioned in Chapter 1. He did not even greet me nor did he ask me about work or my mom, as he always used to do. I had never seen him like that in all the 27 years he had been my doctor. He took my file, opened it and showed me the blood test result and said, "Do you know what shape you are in? You have diabetes. Your condition is very dangerous. You could go into cardiac arrest!"

He then told me that in my situation, the first line of defense was Metformin, and he issued me a three months' prescription. "I want you to take two pills in the morning before breakfast and two in the evening five minutes before dinner." He was not done. "I want you to call this number and make an appointment to see a diabetes nurse at Burnaby General. She will teach you how to manage the diabetes."

During my drive home from his office, I was confused. I hated myself for having behaved in such a way that endangered my life. Two days later, the diagnosis truly began to sink in. I felt horrible and became distraught. I started crying. Adding fuel to the fire of my distress was the fact that I had lost my job in June of that same year and Unemployment Insurance had disqualified me and refused to pay benefits to me. With everything that I was going through emotionally, it was all so overwhelming. The last thing I had needed was to be told that I was a diabetic.

The Power of Denial

Until I experienced it, I never realized really how powerful denial was. I couldn't believe what was happening. Me? A diabetic? I had heard that Blacks were prone to diabetes, but I could not accept my present circumstances or believe they were happening to me. In the past, when I had dealt with people who were in denial in my counselling practice, I could not understand their mindset when something obvious was staring them in the face and yet, they were still able to deny it. For the first time, I was doing the same thing. My mind was closed shut. What I wanted to believe was that none of this was true.

Still in denial, I made an attempt to secure an immediate cure. I couldn't accept my condition. I just couldn't. In the process of seeking a quick cure, first I called the missionaries from The Church of Jesus Christ of Latter Day Saints and asked them to come and give me a blessing so that I could be healed. I talked to three different missionaries, and in the blessings of all three was the same thing. I quote their exact words: "Work with doctors." End quote.

I didn't want to hear what they had to say. I wanted a fast cure—a miracle—anything to rid me of the diabetes. Rather than do what I was asked, out of desperation, I turned to the Internet to look for a cure and became caught up in it rather quickly.

I was quickly exposed to the business of online cures for diabetes. All sorts of people were offering cures. Many had well-scripted sales pages pointing fingers at pharmaceutical companies and saying how terrible they were. Many of these websites claimed that they had a "magic pill" called Banaba that would cure diabetes. Websites had videos of young men claiming to be doctors and declaring that the pills they were selling were an actual cure. I was willing to try anything. Desperation and denial had taken over my ability to think clearly. Another website had a woman who claimed she had cured her husband's type 2 diabetes and their doctor was surprised at how she had done it, but she did not post any blood test results nor mention her husband's doctor's name. Furthermore, the website offered several free products, one of which was an e-book on managing type 2 diabetes. But oh, there is one more thing. She was selling a six-month supply of supplements. The website was so convincing, but just when I was about to order her pills, a thought occurred to me. If the website clearly stated that her supplements could cure type 2 diabetes in 30 days, then why was a six-month purchase required? Also, if her supplements could cure type 2 diabetes, why was she giving away an e-book on *managing* type 2 diabetes? These two thoughts prevented me from giving away my credit card information by making the purchase.

That was not all the deception I faced on the Internet. The next thing I knew, spam email with promises to restore insulin sensitivity by use of a diabetes cure product—cinnamon—began to show up in my Hotmail inbox. A video linked in the emails contained gruesome images of amputated legs, legs with wounds, and small bottles of cinnamon that they wanted their victims to purchase for $16. As an experiment, for several months I added cinnamon to my breakfast. It did absolutely nothing. I felt sad because the person who was on the video claimed that his mission was to heal people. In actuality, his sales pitch caused me to put my life at risk by placing my hope in cinnamon. I then decided to do some research on these people I had encountered on the Internet and others like them. What I found was that there are a multitude of people who find shreds of information about a subject in which they have little or no expertise. Once they find some information they think they can make a profit from, they quickly send out emails en-masse. Through these emails they hope to sell a bogus product and turn a quick profit before they are exposed. In the case I just mentioned, at that time in Europe, cinnamon was being considered for testing to see if it had properties that could help diabetics.

The Blindness Experience

The blindness I underwent was a first-hand experience of not being able to see anything in front of you but a complete blur. When drastic measures had to be taken to bring my blood sugar level down, my doctor prescribed a heavy dose of Metformin, a blood glucose-reducing drug. I took two pills in the morning and two in the evening. Shortly after I began taking the medication, I woke up one morning and everything appeared blurry. I thought it might clear up after some moments, but it didn't happen. I started to panic. I managed to call a friend by feeling out the numbers on my touch phone. I didn't know my doctor's number by heart so I couldn't call him. When my friend came over, I got him to find the number and call the doctor's office.

Since I could only get an appointment for the next day, I just had to manage until the appointment. The next day, all my friends and co-workers were at work, so I decided I would just have to see if I could drive to the doctor's office. Was I concerned that I would crash? Yes! A taxi would have been helpful, but I simply didn't have the money readily available to take a taxi.

I started the car and inched along. I could vaguely make out the images and shapes of buildings and large objects. I couldn't distinguish between male and female. I was not able to read signs. I could see the shapes of cars on the street and the colour of lights. I drove slowly in the slow lane and, amazingly, got there without incident.

When I arrived at the doctor's office, he examined me and proceeded to explain that there had been so much sugar in my body that when the medication began to bring the level down very rapidly, my vision was impacted. He told me that within four weeks, my vision would return. Fortunately for me, he was correct.

Information is Power

I was not the type who could just accept that I had to live with and manage my diabetes for the rest of my life. The only way I could heal myself was to delve into research to allow me get to the bottom of what was going on inside my type 2 diabetic body. I found myself compelled to do the research not to heal just myself, but also for the millions of other diabetics around the world. I was intrigued by the work of Dr. Paula Baillie-Hamilton. As I mentioned previously, she struggled with her weight and dieted, but without success. A study she conducted revealed that obesity in people who cannot lose weight is often caused by toxins. Based on her research findings, Dr. Baillie-Hamilton wrote several books, the one I have mentioned is *Toxic Overload*. One of her major discoveries was that an alteration of fat producing genes is caused by chemicals in our food. The concept that chemicals in our environment could be contributing to the obesity epidemic is often credited to an article Baillie-Hamilton published in the *Journal of Alternative and Complementary Medicine* in 2002. Since then, many studies and related articles have supported her thesis.

The chemicals we consume that cause weight gain have been termed "obesogens." Baillie-Hamilton postulates that these chemicals damage our ability to lose weight and resultantly cause the production of fat. She asserts that this is a main reason for a global obesity epidemic. Obesogens distort the appetite, making us crave unhealthy foods. Adrenaline and dopamine, which help us lose weight, are reduced by obesogens and this adversely affects the metabolism.

Obesogens are "endocrine disruptors" because they obstruct the chemical messaging of hormones to cells. These hormones regulate metabolism, growth, and development. Other hormones negatively impacted are those associated with metabolism. Some obesogens have an impact on the number and size of fat cells. Obesogens are very often found in red meat.

One thing that excited me about Dr. Baillie-Hamilton's approach was that she herself was her main test subject. Inspired by this approach, I undertook my own research to find a way to overcome my diabetes.

In January 2012, I exercised vigorously. Throughout the month, I continued to monitor my blood glucose level each day. It was the first time I felt motivated to do so; I had previously not tracked it daily. I exercised six days a week, both in the morning and in the evening. The maximum acceptable blood sugar level in Canada is 7.0 millimoles per litre (mmol/L) 2 hours after meals, which is equal to approximately 127 milligrams per deciliter (mg/dl) in the US. My hope and efforts were to get my level within that range and get off the medication I was expected to take for the rest of my life.

Besides the exercise, according to extensive research I had done, I put together a supplements program comprised of all of the most proven and efficacious remedies. Also based on my research, I set out a suitable dietary program. Employing these three elements with regularity, I achieved remarkably quick results. After only three weeks, my test results showed a drop from my October 2011 result of 8.4. It was now January 2012, and after having thought I should just give in to managing my diabetes with pharmaceutical drugs, I was down to 6.2—and as I just said and would like to repeat—this was after only three weeks of executing my own reversal and cure program. What impressed me the most was my ACR result, or albumin to creatinine ratio, which was 1.6. An ACR of 1.6 meant that I had absolutely no liver damage as a result of the sugar levels I had for over two years. I had been told that my ACR should not be more than 2 and my blood pressure should be around 120/80 in order to be considered perfectly normal. And yes, when I saw my doctor with my results after following my program, he told me that my blood pressure was just that—120/80. Adding to my joy was the fact that when I had first been diagnosed with diabetes, my waistline was 46 inches. By the end of 2012, I had that measurement down to 33.5 inches, but I still had a goal to get it down to 32 inches, which it was from age 27 until around 40. The image below shows the test results with numbers that I never believed would become a reality when I was diabetic. This marvelous miracle actually occurred because of all I had implemented to reverse my diabetes including the diet, the exercise routine, and the adjustments I made to the supplements I had been taking. The result I attained was a result of acquiring knowledge and application of commitment, and discipline. I had learned that with type 2 diabetes, you have to stay on top of it or it will stay on top of you.

It was on February 1st, 2012 at about 8:45 AM that I left home for my doctor's appointment to go over the blood test results of January 27, 2012.

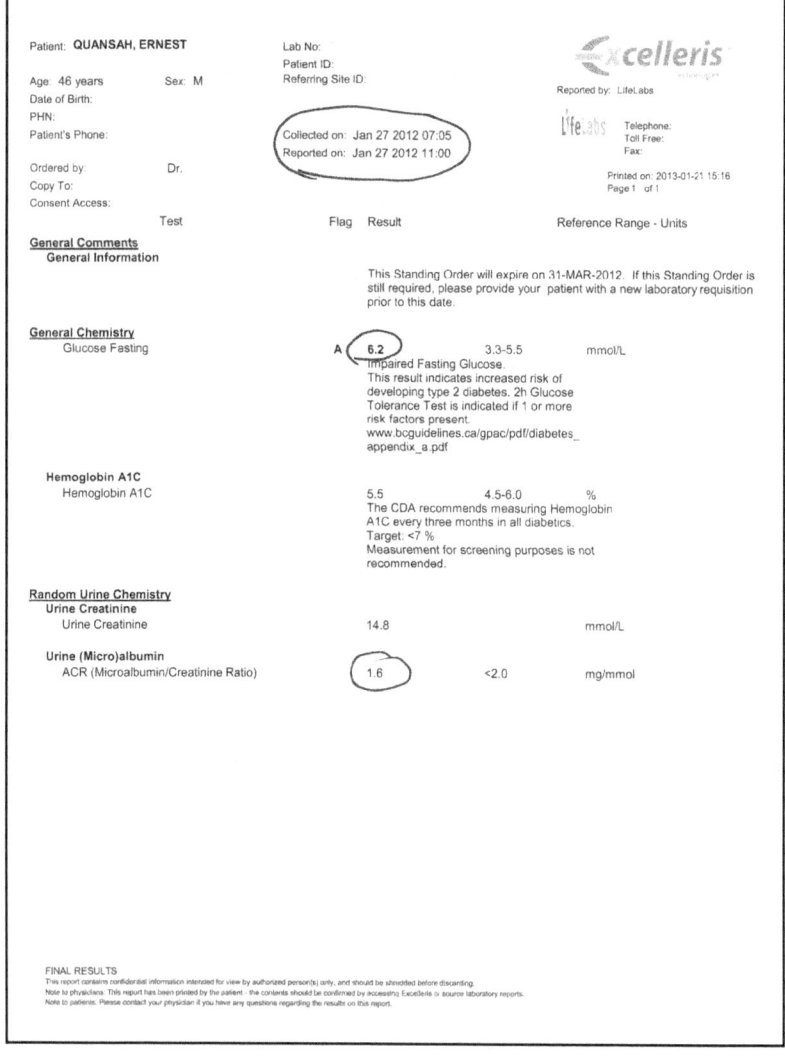

The blood test results of January 27, 2012.

As I sat in his office, I told him that I was feeling stronger and more energetic. I was eating right and I was going to the gym twice a day, six days a week and I had lost another nine pounds. I also told him that three days before, I had not eaten for four hours after breakfast and I had felt slightly lightheaded as a result. I continued my account saying that the next day, I ate breakfast and, after that, I intentionally did not eat for six hours to see how my body would feel. All this was part of my research. Without food for six hours, if I was still a diabetic, I should feel lightheaded and have a lack energy. But I did not feel lightheaded. That same day, when I went to the gym and did some exercise, I quickly felt stronger than before. The day before my visit to the doctor, I had tested myself again. I had breakfast after the gym, then a salad with baked salmon for lunch. I did not eat again until 7 PM and I did not feel light-headed. All this was continued testing that I was conducting on myself as part of my research.

My doctor reviewed my chart and blood test and his eyebrows rose. "Wow, Ernest," he exclaimed. "Your diabetes is gone. Your hemoglobin level is absolutely excellent. Give yourself a pat on the back. I am impressed. I will even give you a hug if you like. Well done. You are one of the very few people I have seen in 40 years who have managed to cure their diabetes." He smiled and said, "Well, I will not say you are cured because a cure means it is gone for good. Now, be careful. Don't go out and start eating a lot and putting on weight. Your diabetes might come back."

"I am actually eating healthy now," I replied, "and I will continue to exercise. My goal is to maintain my weight at where it now is. I will exercise and run 30 minutes, four times a week." I explained to my doctor that I wasn't just eating anything and exercising randomly. I told him I was following a customized routine and a menu cycle accompanied by vitamin/supplement therapy and that I would continue with it.

"That will be good. I will monitor you and if it does not come back, that will mean you are cured. Here, I will give you a copy of the report." And he handed it to me. "Take it, flaunt it. Tell the people at the gym; tell your pharmacist that you are normal. You don't have diabetes anymore." When he said that, I was so, so overjoyed. I have never been that happy. I proceeded to tell him that I kept a journal and was thinking about writing a book about how I reversed my diabetes. The purpose of the book would be to help other diabetics by letting them know that there is a way to reversal and possibly a cure. He replied, "That is an excellent idea." I asked him for a testimonial confirming that my diabetes, even though it was an extreme case, had been reversed. He was happy to issue me a hand-written testimonial for the book I was considering writing.

Good Health Is in the Food We Eat

Before you read my doctor's testimonial, I want to share an experience that a friend of mine had. This friend's mother was about 70 years old and had high cholesterol, asthma, and other conditions. To bring her cholesterol level down, her doctor suggested prescription drugs. My friend asked the doctor if there was a natural way to reduce her mother's cholesterol level. According to the doctor, my friend's mother was old and the only way she could be helped was with the use of drugs. My friend was not willingly to accept the doctor's conclusion. After doing her own research, she put her mother on a diet largely comprised of steamed and baked vegetables. She took her mother off all dairy products, as well as eggs. She replaced her teas with cinnamon tea. After three months, her mother's cholesterol level dropped so low, her mother's doctor asked my friend how she had done it.

All I learned throughout my journey came by means of unprecedented revelations. These included my good fortune in meeting a well-respected researcher from Texas who told me that just by eating raw vegetables every day for three months, your blood can become pure and clear of disease.

We all know that animals in their natural habitat don't get heart conditions, diabetes, or bone cancer. The only animals that acquire these life-threatening diseases are pets fed with man-made, processed foods. Elephants and many other forest animals eat plants, berries, and raw vegetables. Because of their diet, their blood is pure.

Hand-written testimonial by Dr. Anthony Robinson.

In 2017, The Canadian Health minister appealed to Canadians about their eating habits and said that four out of every five Canadians are at risk of becoming diabetic. Her statement implies that diabetes can be acquired through lifestyle choices.

Returning back to my visit with my doctor: Once he had given me the exceptional news that I was diabetes-free, he walked me to the door. As we approached the reception area, I felt like I was in a dream. I couldn't believe what I had achieved. In the same way that the news took time to sink in on the day I was diagnosed as diabetic, the new diagnosis had not fully sunk in. One of the receptionists was standing in the hallway doing something. My doctor told her, "Congratulate this man." When we reached the reception area, he showed the receptionists my very first blood test results from when I became a diabetic saying to them, "Congratulate this man. Look at his first test result, when I first diagnosed him two years ago. And look at his test result now. He is free from diabetes. What a great job." He turned to me, smiling. "I am so proud of you." He made me a copy of the test results and handed them to me. When I left his office, I drove straight to my pharmacist and told him the good news. He and others in his store were overjoyed for me. "Congratulations, man. I told you type 2 diabetes can be reversed," said my pharmacist.

I am living proof that diabetes can be reversed, despite the level of sugar in the body. I accomplished this successfully—*so can you.*

Everything happens for a reason. My experiences and this book were meant to happen. I believe this. I also believe that this book is needed in order to show that, regardless of how bad your type 2 diabetes is, you can restore your insulin sensitivity and return to normal health.

Three Powerful Proofs Showing that Diabetes Type 2 Can Be Reversed

The first proof I would like to present is this: The efficacy of my research in helping diabetics heal was reviewed in 2016 by Brunilda Nazario, MD, *WebMD*, Chief Medical Editor, and was featured in the magazine *WebMD Diabetes,* fall 2016 issue, page 19. The article was titled *Chef Reveals His Secrets for Reversing Diabetes*. WebMD, made up of hundreds of physicians, provides health care information to medical doctors, as well as to the general public, including diabetics.

The second proof is this: In addition to the above mentioned *WebMD* article, there is research that confirms that customized diet and an exercise plan like the one I put together after my research can reverse type 2 diabetes. Here is the URL to the related article: http://www.nationalpost.com/m/wp/health/blog.html?b=news.nationalpost.com/health/type-2-diabetes-can-be-cured-in-four-months-if-you-cut-calories-and-exercise-research-shows

Here is the final proof: The International Diabetes Federation is an organization whose mission is to promote diabetes care and cure. Their Director of Policy and Programmes, Dr. David Cavan, released his own recipe book for diabetics, which is intended to help them reverse diabetes.

Recipe books used without the accompaniment of exercise and supplements offer a very low-percentage possibility of bringing about the reversal of diabetes (depending on the severity of the condition in the individual). Recipes books—or diet alone—is beneficial for those who are pre-diabetic. Based on my research, evidence shows that for reversal to occur, (especially in more severe cases,) the combination of proper diet and customized exercise is most efficacious in bringing about reversal. This fact is supported by the research published in *The Telegraph* and re-published in the

National Post. Still, Dr. Cavan's position as a leading figure in the International Diabetes Federation, and the fact that he has written a recipe book to help diabetics heal, confirms the assumption that diabetes type 2 can be reversed.

The Benefit of Decisiveness

I asked a question earlier which was this: Why do we make decisions or do things that hurt us? Here is my next question: If you are diabetic, how would your life change if you put in efforts to reverse and cure your diabetes and you were successful? Would you feel happiness, healed, healthy, and cured? Would you avoid the tragic outcomes of limb amputation, liver failure, and heart disease? If we can make decisions that hurt us, it means we can also make decisions that result in the opposite outcome. There are multiple benefits when a diabetic does the required exercises and follows the required diet for bringing about the reversal and cure of their condition. Some of these benefits include normalizing of blood pressure and decrease of the bad cholesterol (LDL) level.

Some statements my doctor made on the day he declared me healed from my diabetes were these: "You don't have high blood sugar. You're in excellent health." How would you feel upon hearing your own doctor utter these words?

Just as we make decisions that make us become diabetic, so too can we make decisions that bring us back to good health.

Type 2 Diabetes Education

Sometimes, information disseminated by those working in a trusted profession can be misleading or give people a false sense of good health. It has been said that diabetes affects certain races more than others. According to this theory, the level of predominance of those falling victim to diabetes follows this order: Blacks, First Nation people, Hispanics, Asians, and finally, Causations. But this conclusion seems to be changing. Increasingly, many Caucasians, including children, are becoming diabetic. In fact, any time I hear diabetes spoken of in the health news, the group that seems to have the largest increase in cases is the Caucasian race. This calls into question the notion that type 2 diabetes predominantly affects Blacks, Asians, and Aboriginals. There is currently no evidence that this is the case. In countries such as Norway, diabetes is becoming more and more common, and the citizens of that nation are largely Caucasian with very white skin. Acquiring diabetes is not determined by race. Aside from poor diet and lack of exercise, lack of exposure to sunshine causing a vitamin D deficiency is also a contributor to the onset of diabetes.

Diabetes and Obesity

It has been said that when people become obese, they could become diabetic. The problem with this statement is that I know countless obese men and women who are not diabetic. Similarly, I know thin people who are diabetic. I have said before that most type 2 diabetics are diagnosed when they are in their mid-forties. We now know that children as young as 12 years are now being diagnosed with the condition.

One thing that obese people, people living in tropical countries, and children diagnosed with diabetes all have in common is the consumption of refined sugar, sweet soft drinks, and processed foods. More and more officials in our government health departments have stated that the acquisition of diabetes has a direct relationship with the food people eat.

According to Jeffrey Smith, a leading consumer advocate at the Institute of Responsible Technology, many doctors in the US recommend that their patients stay away from genetically modified foods. It is believed that many of these patients have recovered from certain chronic diseases. Evidence shows that diabetes is very much related to our food choices, or should I say, the foods we are forced to eat? Here is a comparison that explains why I say, "The foods we are *forced* to eat." We are told that we have freedom of speech, yet when one dares to speak out against unhealthy food products and the giant food corporations who manufacture them, the corporations go on the defense and threaten to sue just so that they can continue to sell their toxic food products. We end up at the doctor's office and the government pays for the treatment. It seems to me that even governments are being bullied into submission.

Health Problems Triggered by Type 2 Diabetes

Impotence

High levels of sugar in the body can cause impotence in men. Shortly after I was diagnosed, a large boil grew on the back of my head and some even appeared on intimate parts of my body. My doctor informed me it was because of the excess sugar in my body.

Blindness

In developing nations where there is less education on diabetes, many victims of this condition lose their eyesight.

Neuropathy

Nerve damage is another result of type 2 diabetes, if nothing is done to reverse it.

Diabetic Ulcers

Many people know about leg amputation due to diabetes. Diabetes ulcers are open sores that can lead to infection and in severe cases, leg amputation.

Heart Disease

If I had not done anything to reverse my condition, it could have caused heart disease. The nurses at the clinic I was sent for treatment early on made this very clear to me.

Kidney & Liver Disease

Just as sugar can cause heart disease, it can also cause kidney or liver diseases. To sum up, sugar buildup can destroy your internal organs, period.

I will now put my latest question a different way: With all this information and education on diabetes at one's finger tips, why would a diabetic make decisions that would hurt him or her?

Don't Let Diabetes Control You

In 2015, I was speaking with a longtime friend and pharmaceutical researcher working for a US drug company. He told me that he was going to stop smoking that very day. I was not so sure that he could accomplish what he had set out to do. I reminded him that he had said he would stop smoking several times over the years that I had known him. He never did stop so how was he going to stop now? This was his reply, "I cannot do this anymore. I have a Ph.D. and feel like the cigarettes are controlling my life. Whenever the thought of smoking comes into my mind, I go outside to smoke. The cigarettes are controlling me. I am going to take control of my life starting today." He then disposed of his pack of cigarettes and has never smoked again. His face has cleared up. He looks more vibrant now than he did when he smoked. He is no longer a slave to cigarettes, which were poisoning him and killing him slowly.

I don't see reversible diabetes any differently. When I was suffering from the condition, I saw it as enslaving and controlling my life and knew that at some point, it would progress to type 1 diabetes, the incurable type. In the meantime, I would wait for it to unleash numerous diseases before it would take my life. But then I decided that it was my life and my body and I had to take control of both.

Telling diabetics that they cannot do anything about their condition other than live with it and manage it is dishonest and allows the diabetes to control its victim. This control takes on different forms. I once spoke with some diabetes bloggers about my article on diabetes which was featured in *WebMD*. I assumed that the bloggers would be excited. Some of them said that the only way they would re-publish the article was if I used the word "manage" in the title instead of "reverse." The American Diabetes Association also has their own online magazine, as do many others in the diabetes industry. All refused to let their readers know that type 2 diabetes can be reversed, as featured in *WebMD Diabetes*. These refusals led me to do an investigation. I discovered one common thread. Those I had reached out to, all of whom refused to share my story, either sold advertising space on their blogs or received some funding from diabetes drug manufacturers. Some diabetes websites in the UK are partners with Abbott Diabetes Care (blood glucose meter suppliers) and ask you to fill out a form in order to get free blood glucose meters.

Diabetics that accept when they are told that they can only manage their condition are responsible for allowing themselves to be treated such, because they don't want to listen or take the necessary action that could heal them in two to four months (and even less time, as in my case). They are willing to live life in a manner that will eventually destroy them. How we treat ourselves is a clear indication of how we fell about ourselves.

A Matter of Desperation

Diet pill peddlers accuse drug companies of intentionally hooking diabetics on drugs and on blood sugar monitors out of greed, while keeping the truth that there is a cure a secret. Though they are largely correct, these diet pill peddlers are the worst misleaders of diabetics. At least the pills sold by drug companies are prescribed by doctors and the patients are monitored. Supplements and diet pills touted to cure diabetes, which are sold by greedy, heartless individuals whose contact information is not available on their websites is the worst deception. What method do these people use to fortify their sales pitches? They always say, "As seen on CNN" or "as seen on TV." "As seen on CNN" or "TV" has become a very convincing marketing trick used by many website owners. Okay, we think, *if their product was on CNN, it must be good.*

Such scams are so widespread that on December 28th, 2012, Dr. Oz did a show on health food stores that use his name on products to make sales. In addition, on Friday, January 4th, 2013 the news program *20/20* mentioned the extent to which many websites are using the type of sales pitch I have just indicated. *20/20* went even further by pointing out how the picture of a beautiful woman who was once a news reporter in France has been used to promote and sell acai berry as a weight-loss product. It does not stop there.

A promotional article about this former news reporter from France was made by the scammers claiming that acai berry worked so well for this woman that she wrote a "tell all" article with this claim. Yet, on this *20/20* show, the woman said she had neither given her name nor her picture to be used, nor had she written the article to sell the product.

The extent to which some people are willing to go in order to take consumers' money is astounding. I will end this rant by asking another question? Why do some people and companies do things to consumers knowing very well that they are hurting them? Regarding the pill peddlers on the Internet, the answer is obvious. Regarding the companies selling these unproven cure products, their commitment is not to those they sell their products to, but to their investors.

Type 2 diabetes can never ever be reversed by taking any of these kinds of pills because they cannot reverse the body's insulin resistance. I have explained earlier what that is and what its effects are.

Research on Reversing Type 2 Diabetes

I WAS WORKING AS a chef and also a part-time relationship coach after I completed a one-year Peer Counselling certificate program at the University of British Columbia. My research was well underway. Just like many a type 2 diabetic seeking to heal, I began with going to the gym, though I wasn't following any set exercise routine nor was I following any set of menus for diet. What my program included was eating the foods and doing the things the nurses at the diabetes clinic I went to after being diagnosed had advised. This included going for a 20-minute walk after each meal. It also included taking the vitamins they suggested. When I was faced with little change in my condition, I reviewed what I had been doing to see where I could improve. My review revealed that

I was not following a sufficiently good diet. I was still eating some sweets—not a lot—but some. I went to see my doctor for his advice. When he came into the examination room he asked, "What can I do for you today?"

As I have already told you, I asked Dr. Robinson if type 2 diabetes could be cured and I was encouraged and inspired by his affirmative response. He did not tell me exactly what exercise to do or what meals to eat. He simply said, "You have to exercise like crazy—and those chocolates that you have been eating—stop! It can be done, but it is very difficult." He further told me that two percent of diabetics are able to cure their diabetes.

I thought, *Difficult? What was that supposed to mean? Was he trying to tell me that I couldn't do it? If only two percent of type 2 diabetics are able to reverse their condition, then could I be one person out of that two percent?*

Armed with the information that only two percent of diabetics are able to reverse their condition, I knew I wanted to be part of that successful minority. Thoughts raced through my mind as I left his office. During the drive home, I talked to myself. *I must do this. This diabetes has got to go. I don't care how. It's got to go.* In the following days, I put together my first type 2 diabetes reversal plan based on the research I had been doing.

I realized something. If it were true that type 2 diabetes could be reversed or cured, and that it was very difficult, as my doctor told me, then the secret to curing or reversing diabetes must be discipline. As encouraged as I felt by this revelation, part of me was concerned. *What if I am stuck with this type 2 diabetes forever? Maybe, just maybe, it is hard work to reverse type 2 diabetes. Maybe it is too hard for me.*

A pressing concern that I struggled with was this: The diabetes did not give me any pain whatsoever, but it was still a silent killer.

The way I saw it, if it could kill me in my sleep or cause me to go into a cardiac arrest, then yes, it was dangerous, period.

I pondered these dangers coupled with what many doctors had said, as well as the Canadian Diabetic Association website, that type 2 diabetes is a progressive condition, meaning it will eventually become type 1 diabetes, the deadly type. With these thoughts, I had reason to take my condition very seriously.

Why Type 2 Diabetes May Fail to Be Cured

There are four reasons why, in my opinion, diabetes is difficult to reverse:

1. **Information:** The information to reverse and cure type 2 diabetes is available but difficult to find because it is not made available to diabetics in its entirety.

2. **Lack of knowledge and action:** The second problem is that while the information to reverse diabetes is available, most diabetics and non-diabetics alike don't acquire the knowledge or take action.

3. **Lack of effort:** My doctor was right when he said it was difficult to cure diabetes. Many diabetics don't make the required effort to heal themselves. Others continue to eat the wrong foods and live a lifestyle that makes it difficult for them to reverse their condition.

4. **Eating Habits:** Any time I see type 2 diabetics who are not able to cure their condition, I notice that they are eating all the wrong foods, including having sweetened drinks. In mid-January 2013, Dr. Sanjay Gupta of CNN did a piece on popular soda drinks where he showed that one can of

a sweetened soda drink contains nine teaspoons of sugar. Another reporter did a piece on another popular soft drink, which has a lot of sugar per can. I see many type 2 diabetics eating starchy foods; like pasta, potatoes, and bread, and washing them down with sweetened soda drinks. It seems to me that some type 2 diabetics don't really get the message as to why they cannot cure themselves and others simply don't care. The State of New York has put a ban on supersized soda drinks. Even with all the information we are privy to regarding our health, some people laugh at the health ideas that are put forward. Some news channels go on and on about how people's right to decide what to eat and drink is being taken from them. In 2013, I found information showing that processed food manufacturers continue to design their food products to make the consumer want to eat more and more. They achieve this by finding the perfect combination of sugar, salt, and fat, and use those constituents in their products to trigger the brain to want more. Their own researchers and scientists who develop these products refer to the point where you will crave for more as the "bliss point." They know the harm their processed foods can cause, yet they are determined to get consumers to eat more of them. And many consumers don't care. I am not surprised that food manufacturers are growing their profits even when a US government report has stated that processed foods are worse than fatty foods; they cause inflammation and contribute to type 2 diabetes and heart conditions.

Why My Type 2 Diabetes Persisted

I researched and read until I learned the underlying cause of type 2 diabetes. Many experts do believe that type 2 diabetes is caused by poor diet, lack of exercise, and the excessive consumption of sugar and processed food. October 4, 2013, the programme *Market Place* did a show on which a Dr. Robert Lustig asserted that sugar causes diabetes. He is not the only one who has made this assertion. Sugar has been defined by many doctors as a poison. Sugar is made up of two compounds: glucose and fructose. When consumed, the glucose is used for energy while the fructose turns into fat. The fat builds up around the internal organs, including the pancreas, and finds its way into the blood stream and coats the blood cells, preventing them from absorbing and transporting sugar to the muscles to be used as energy. It is fructose that causes belly fat. Now here is the kicker. It has been said that since 1999, executives of the processed food industry have known about the health-damaging effects caused by sugar for a very long time. Tests have shown these effects. The processed food company executives hate to hear these facts. Adding insult to injury, in my view, is the fact that a researcher discovered the bliss point and the food industry continues to abuse it. In simple English, they produce food that is addictive. How is this any different from the cigarette industry?

Reversing Type 2 Diabetes—My Second Attempt

With much more information in hand, I continued on with my research into how type diabetes can be reversed. I put hour upon hour and day upon day into this research. At one point, I really thought I was on my way to getting rid of the diabetes. But this second attempt failed as well, despite all that I had learned. I had modified my diet and taken all the sugar out, but I was still eating rice and some desserts—when I had dinner with friends—which I did on a weekly basis. Yes, I would have some cookies and some sweet drinks in small amounts. I went to the gym and ran on the treadmill for 20 minutes a day. All this, yet I was still diabetic. I must say that I was feeling a little better, but it turned out that everything I was doing was simply helping me *manage* my type 2 diabetes. I was very frustrated. I wanted to quit, but as I've said, I could not settle for just managing my diabetes. It had to go, period.

Reversing Type 2 Diabetes—My Third Attempt

By this time, it was already the beginning of January 2012. More than two years had passed since my diagnosis. I upped the research. Early one morning while I was in bed reading, I began to ponder. A light went on in my head when this occurred to me: Since type 2 diabetes is caused when our bodies become insulin resistant, then what I need to do is restore my body's insulin sensitivity.

That very moment was an awakening. I could feel something. *This was it*. I had stumbled on how type 2 diabetes can be reversed. I had been focusing on curing my diabetes instead of finding the root cause and fixing that. I began to feel it. I could feel that the diabetes was soon to be finished—banished from my body. I researched how I could restore my body's insulin sensitivity. It turned out that what prevented me from success during the first two trials was that I had gone about the research in the wrong way.

For several days, from morning until night, I remained absorbed in my research. I made another appointment with my doctor. This time when I went to see him, I asked him point blank, "How do I cure my diabetes?"

He said, "Type 2 diabetes can be cured with a number of methods all working together." This statement was followed by a series of recommendations: "Take sugar out of your diet. No cookies, no processed foods, no candy bars, no donuts, no chocolates."

What my doctor told me that day was exactly what I had been reading about during the final stages of my research. After that visit, I went home and put together a program that was not about an external cure, but was instead, a plan to restore my body's insulin sensitivity. This would necessarily include a *customized* exercise routine, not just going to the gym and randomly doing whatever exercise I wanted to do. This was also the time when my training as a chef kicked in. For the diet part, I created a delicious, customized menu and created a cycle with the various elements of the menu. I would do the exercise routines at particular times and eat at particular times. On February 19th of 2012, exactly 21 days after I started the new plan I had put together, I was pronounced type 2 diabetes-FREE. Just as the news of my diagnosis had made me numb, on this day, the good news made me numb again. It felt like a dream. Though I had accomplished what I had set out to, I still could not believe that I had succeeded. What added to my surprise was how quickly I had reversed my diabetes—21 days! I wanted every single type 2 diabetic and non-diabetic alike to learn about this.

Diabetes and Your Blood Cells

Diabetes can be triggered when the white blood cell count is very low, according to many diabetes specialist doctors. So, refined sugar alone is not the culprit. There is also stress. Thus, I knew I had to take time to relax if I wanted to reduce the amount of stress caused by my life. Stress reduces our white blood cell count. It makes our hair go from its natural color to grey. I witnessed this for myself as I began to feel the stress at work and in my life. My hair changed quickly from silky black to grey on the sides of my head.

Look at pictures of presidents before their presidency and compare them to photos taken one year later. Their hair has usually gone gray after just one year in office. Whenever I am interviewed for management positions, I always say there is no such thing as a difficult job. Difficulties in the workplace always seem to be because of the staff: the problems and the toxic atmosphere they create.

Don't Be Deceived!

TYPE 2 DIABETES is like obesity: it can lead to discouragement and low self-esteem. Anyone who knows a lot about weight-loss products knows that TV ads and infomercials often use words that target low self-esteem. *"Are you overweight?" "Being fat stinks!"* etc. These phrases humiliate obese individuals and result in an even lower self-image than they already had, so that the guilt will cause them to purchase the weight-loss products—most of which don't work. Take the "Ab Circle." The infomercial for this product was based on an outright lie, like almost all the products out there for obesity. The creators of this product have been ordered to return over 10 million dollars to their customers because of false representation. The BBC has reported that data from adults in 186 countries showed that the number of obese people worldwide rocketed from

105 million in 1975 to 641 million in 2014—about a 500% increase. I can speak from experience that diabetes causes low self-esteem and discouragement. Reversing it results in the experience of these psychological changes:

- One becomes much happier.
- One regains self-esteem.
- One's confidence increases tenfold.
- One may feel like he or she can accomplish anything.
- One feels more relaxed without the concerns about diabetes constantly at the back of one's mind.

My Role as an Advocate

As Nelson Mandela once said, "It is the power of the people that causes change." To cause change I had to start with myself, the consumer. Now in my journey, I find myself an advocate for change. In the past 10 years, almost everywhere I have worked, I have had to stand up for the staff. In some cases, staff members have approached me and asked me to file a complaint to get the boss fired. I have gotten two of my bosses fired. I mentioned one of them in the opening chapter. It is my pleasure to advocate for diabetics. Type 2 diabetes and obesity is said to affect people with a lesser education, according to the University of Spain. Their finding is based on the purchasing behavior they found among consumers, which was that less educated people are less likely to read labels on ready-to-eat-processed foods before purchase in comparison to those with higher education. Consumers have enormous buying power. Manufacturers of food products maintain that they are not responsible for obesity. They say consumers have the power of choice to use their money whichever way they want. The fact is that the consumer is given two choices with their purchasing power; either to buy foods that support life or to buy foods that cause death. In the supermarket, if ready-to-eat food items were labeled *Eat this and it will make you fat and diabetic*, one wouldn't buy those products, but would probably warn family and friends about them. But the reality is that every day, a multitude of consumers eat these harmful foods of their own accord. Food manufacturers and the food industry as a whole are not as powerful as we are led to believe. It is you, the consumer that has the power. It is up to you how you use it.

Putting a Financial Strain on the Health Budget

Our choices affect family, friends, and even people we don't know. In December 2012, a report came out in Canada saying that people in chronic pain are now being sent to therapists to learn meditation in order to relieve the pain. The program is working and the US government is now also looking into how meditation relieves pain.

I had never seriously considered how one's choices affect the government until I began this line of research. I have often wondered: If people were to live a healthy lifestyle, how many billions of dollars would they help the government health system save? In most developed nations, there is enough money to allow the government to provide good services to their citizens. Often, it is the citizens whose lifestyle choices significantly strain the budget set aside for health services. As it stands, money spent in developed nations on diabetes is in the billions.

At one point, the guilt of wasting tax payers' money caught up to me. Each time I went to the diabetes clinic or went to the lab to do a blood glucose test—all at the cost of the government—I felt that guilt. Having medical insurance did not make me feel better about the choices I had made that led to my circumstance. All the money my diabetes extracted from the government could have been used to improve infrastructure, recreational facilities, and medical services, or to build academic institutions and support essential social services.

Governments and diabetes researchers could benefit our society greatly by investing in research and promoting diabetes prevention, care, and cure. Pharmaceutical companies manufacturing diabetes medications have a responsibility to their investors, and so, are only concerned about spending on research that will yield financial gain. If there is no money in a venture, they don't want to be involved in it.

The Word "Free"

The initial concept of this book was of a research project studying diabetes. It had not occurred to me that the journey would take me down this road—the road of uncovering how consumers are conned out of their money. These days, the magic word used for ripping off consumers is the word "free." Many product salespeople, (including those calling themselves doctors and selling diet pills,) have gotten into the act with the tactic of offering "free" products. The scam works because some people don't want to take the time to think carefully about the ads they come across and they simply get enticed by the word "FREE."

Unethical business practices have become so common that companies will blatantly lie to sell their products and services. One of my favorite TV shows is CBC's *Marketplace*. They once did a show called *The Worst Cell Phone Bill*. All three of the major cell phone companies in Canada were caught for their involvement in some sort of fraud. In the CBC programme, they reported the story of a Virgin Mobile customer that was almost brought to tears. The customer's bill was over $4,000 dollars, and Virgin Mobile demanded that the customer pay the amount in full. When the phone company realized that they had been exposed on a TV show, they quickly changed their story saying that the overcharge was due to a satellite-related technical glitch.

The deceptive practices never seem to stop despite a lot of empty rhetoric made by the governments' consumer protection agencies. The average person does not realize that companies spend billions of dollars in research to find out how to sell to consumers. In other words, they do research to find consumer weaknesses and use those weaknesses in order to increase sales. Take diabetes and obesity as examples. Companies that market to this segment of our society know that both obese people and diabetics avoid exercise, for the most part, and want an easy solution to their problems, so many companies come up with products that they claim will help these people achieve their health and fitness goals.

We have all heard of antidepressants that turn out to be catalysts for increased depression. Still, the pharmaceutical companies pour money into alluring victims of depression into using their products. Separately, there is the example of a shoe company that lied in an ad saying that their shoes could help with weight loss. When the US government caught them, they were ordered to refund the consumers almost 40 million dollars.

We Are at War with Greed

In today's world of advanced technology and medicine, it is *not* reasonable to accept the results of research funded by diabetes drug manufacturers, since the companies themselves don't acknowledge that type 2 diabetes is reversible. This information is purposely and intentionally kept away from reaching consumers.

A number of years ago, a report came out of the University of British Columbia stating that drug companies were intentionally selling drugs that consumers did not need. That report got me thinking. I saw an ad telling me to take an antacid before eating to prevent heartburn. I thought, 'I almost never get heartburn unless I eat pasta with meat sauce, but even then, I don't always get heart burn after eating those foods. So why should I *always* take an antacid drug before I eat them when I know that I will not *always* get heartburn?' Some product salespeople believe most consumers don't really think. I wonder why that is?

When a company gives away free kits to diabetics through a hospital in exchange for the diabetic's personal information, it is unethical and wrong, particularly when the patient is not told what will be done with their personal information—and yet it happens all the time. For example, when I was diagnosed, I was sent to the diabetes clinic in our general hospital to learn how to manage the condition. What I was not aware of was that several drug companies had already infiltrated the hospital. How these companies had managed to penetrate a government-run general hospital perplexes me. The clinic had us fill out a form. What we were not told was that the form was going to be sent off to another company without our permission. After we filled out the form, we were each given a small package, which I assumed was a diabetes kits being given to us by the clinic. The gifts included a tiny tube of Colgate toothpaste, a blood monitor and needles, an ad for Viagra, and a number of things not worth mentioning. At the time, I didn't know what was going on.

A year later, I received a call from the U.K. The person had an English accent. He asked to speak with Ernest and I acknowledged that it was he who was speaking. I still remember the conversation as if it happened yesterday: "I am calling to find out how the blood glucose meter is working for you."

For a minute, I was puzzled. When my mind settled, I asked, "What blood glucose meter? Who are you and how did you get my phone number? It is not listed."

"I am calling from Abbot Diabetic Care," he replied. I paused. I was trying to think of what this Abbot Diabetic Care was. Then I realized what had happened. The diabetic clinic at the general hospital had given my personal information to this company.

"I don't appreciate you calling me with this sort of question," I told him. Sensing that I was not pleased with his phone call, the man interrupted and informed me that I didn't have to continue speaking. I asked him never to call me again and hung up the phone.

I went online and googled Abbott Diabetes Care. They make blood glucose meters and provide them free to newly diagnosed diabetics in exchange for personal information given to them by the clinics. This is all done without the diabetic person's knowledge. It was they who had provided the general hospital with the free blood glucose meters we were given in exchange for our personal information. All the hospital had to do was be honest and I probably would have consented to them giving my personal information to another company.

This sort of unethical practice can be found amongst medical doctors, as well. One of my places of employment once requested that I do a TB test. I was given a Tuberculin Skin Test (TST,) a test by which a health care provider injects a liquid (tuberculin) into the skin of the lower part of the arm. In the following visit, I was told that I tested positive. I told the nurse that my boss and I were having a conversation about the TB test and my boss said that the injection is a small dose of TB. The nurse replied, "Tell your boss to mind his own business." She was offended. Now I had to see the medical doctor. She was a young lady. She told me that because my TB test result was positive, she wanted me to take certain medications. She said they were vitamins. It was going to cost me 70 dollars. She scheduled me to return to see her three months later. The following week, I took that prescription to my doctor and asked him about it. What I had been prescribed was not vitamins; it was a steroid that was being tested. My doctor strongly advised me not to touch it because the side effect could be adverse. This pretty lady doctor had lied to me. Three months later, the TB clinic called. I explained my displeasure to the caller letting her know I did not appreciate being lied to and used as part of an experiment.

Each year, new blood glucose meters come on the market. Some can be plugged into a computer. Some companies extol the abilities of their dual-reading meters. Diabetics are intentionally victimized and brainwashed so that they settle for blood glucose meters rather than being given a programme to reverse their condition. Companies do this to harness the customer for making a profit. How can this practice be considered ethical? Even the man from Abbott Diabetic Care knew that contacting me was wrong.

Money Grab

"Money grab" is a milder way of saying con jobs. The practice is so wide spread that it is not uncommon to hear about companies taking advantage of their customers. Banks add additional service fees and say that they have done nothing wrong after they have forced these fees on their customers. When customers ask to have their accounts closed—as they should under the circumstances—the banks back down on the extra charges. Companies that receive government funding—tax payers' money—give hundreds of thousands of the tax payers' money to their top executives as pay increases and bonuses. When a US cell company made an attempt to bring its service to Canada, Canadian cell companies put out a TV ad saying the America companies will increase prices and take other actions that will hurt Canadian companies. What these Canadian cell phone companies were doing was blocking the US companies from coming here and through competition, bringing cell phone usage prices down. The government is not particularly interested in fixing these problems. I once heard a radio ad for acai berry (a product I mentioned earlier which is supposed to boost the immune system). It was being offered for free, so I called to ask about it. When I asked if it was free, as stated in their ad, the customer service agent would not answer my question. When I pressed on, the agent told me, "Sir, after you receive the product, if you don't call to cancel within 14 days, we will send you more, and charge your credit card." Funny, she said that I had to call within 14 days when it takes up to four weeks for the product to arrive. By the time the product was likely to arrive, they would have started charging my credit card and sending me more acai berry. It seems to me that some companies carefully plan to get the consumer's credit card on file so that they can milk the customer.

If there are any small business owners I will avoid at all costs, it is those who offer their services and start by saying that they are a friend. I was once on a visit home with two other men. While I was there, I said I was writing a book on how diabetes can be reversed. The guy whose home we were at whose name was Hannu replied, "If you are writing a book on diabetes, it means you are going to be rich." He added that I would need a website for my book. Within days, I was contacted by Hannu who insisted that he could build me the website. Once I had explained to him the caliber of website that I wanted, he pressed on and told me that we are friends and that I should cancel my agreement with the person that I had already selected to build the website and let him do it instead. Hannu was an acquaintance but not friend. I thought I could trust him, so I gave him the project. He demanded half of the money up front. Before he completed the website, he demanded the other half saying he would not complete the website without this advance payment. I went ahead and gave him the money. He told me that I should not yet look at the website. He, Hannu, said he would take care of everything so that I could concentrate on my writing. He completed a pretty website that fooled me by its looks, but it turned out it was not functional.

Once he understood that I was intending to do to something about the matter, he begged me not take action against him or take him to court and that I would do the right thing. I gave him the chance to fix the website but he could not fix the problems. The things he agreed to do that were most important to me, such as optimizing the website, adding Google Maps, etc., were not done.

To make a long story short, he told me one lie after another. It turned out that he had asked me not to look at the website because I would find out that it did not work. With a background in counselling, I realized that I possibly had another person with psychopathic tendencies on my hands, so I set up a little test. Psychopaths only confess to wrongdoing if they think they will not be held accountable. I sent Hannu an email which said that he could keep the money and that I had long moved on. Within five minutes, he wrote back saying that when he turned the website over to me, it was not complete. Hannu continued, "But I will not refund your money because I don't like being told what to do." Other times, he justified his behavior saying that he had eight children to feed and would not refund my money. The worst part was when he offered to send website traffic my way. I hoped that he might actually be a good person, at heart, and I had maybe misjudged him. He informed me that he had created a program that took content from websites and posted it to Twitter and that he had teamed up with a young lady who was in charge of this operation. He asked for $250 a month for the service, told me that he was only taking on 10 clients, and that there were only two spots left. He explained that if I didn't sign up then, the two spots would soon be taken and it could be another six months before a spot opened. I went ahead and gave him some money for this. After he received the money, he called to tell me that I needed to write an article from which he would extract keywords and post them to Twitter. I said, "But you told me that you have developed a program that goes to my website and takes relevant keywords and posts them to Twitter."

He replied, "It will be better if you write an article containing keywords." I found out within a week that this young woman he had teamed up with was his wife whom he had convinced to quit her job to work with him. He had lied to me again and the service he offered was a scam.

I was very emotionally traumatized. Before letting Hannu build me a website, I explained to him that I wanted to work with diabetics. In the process, I hoped to make a little money to be able to marry my fiancé. This con artist had stood in front of me and his wife and said he would help me by building me the site I had envisioned with all the functionality I needed. His promises all turned out to be deceit.

Here is the story of another lesson I learned: I paid a PR company to send out letters to 200 book stores in the US, Canada, Australia, and New Zealand announcing the release of the first version of my book. The problem was that the website Hannu had built which provided information on my book did not work. As a result, someone wrote an article about me saying that I was a fraud who was linked to a known Russian con artist. I could say it was my fault. I had the most terrible feeling about this Hannu person who sometimes called his website Atuzee Pro, Atuzee, Zufu or The Zufu. I had a very strange feeling that went on for three days, still I went ahead and allowed him to work on my project because in my mind I thought, 'What kind of human being will treat you as a friend and then defraud you?' If you have ever dealt with a person with psychopathic tendencies, you will know that they don't care about hurting people. They tell one lie after another and even if they are caught, they continue until they have drawn their victims into their lies. They know what they are doing. They plan how to do terrible things to people and go as far as to plan how they will defend themselves if caught. The sad part is that despite knowing what they are doing is wrong, they don't stop hurting others. While this may appear as an attack or a rant, it is an experience that needs to be told because such people are classified as some of the most dangerous people in the world. They know they are liars, but in their minds the lies they tell are truth. This to me is what made Hannu a dangerous person. If sharing my experience saves one person from going through a similar experience, I will feel that I have contributed something. When I went to law enforcement to report Hannu, I was told that he had done similar things to others. They told me that people like him con others for a living. They know how the law works. They know that they will not be arrested if they con a person when they are providing some sort service.

    When I authored the first version of this book, I experienced much grief. My problems continued even after the entire Hannu experience. I ended up with someone named Sheldon who said he could fix the website. Sheldon was supposed to replace the content on the site and fix other problems. It turned out that he was broke.

He began to demand that I have him build a new website. Realizing that he was broke, I wanted to help him. So when I purchased a new desktop, I asked him to come and set it up for me so that he could make a little money. While he was setting up the computer, I went into the kitchen and made him dinner. He was happy. When he was done, he took a small gadget out of his pocket for processing a transaction and demanded payment on the spot. When he processed the payment, the screen on the gadget said "approved." Sheldon said the payment hadn't gone through. He then showed me a second gadget saying that if the payment had gone through it would be indicated on this second gadget. In this way, he entered the payment three times and finally said the payment had gone through.

The next day, I gave him a small project. I told him, "Sheldon, since you are fixing the problems on the website, can you please add this one more page to the site and also set the DNS? DNS means Domain Name System, a service that translates domain names into IP addresses; a number code for your website domain name. It is rather easy to input this information, but I wanted Sheldon to do it so that I could give him a little more money for his sustenance. That is when things began to go downhill. He informed me that to set the DNS, it takes 30 minutes and as for adding one more page to my website, he needed to create a template first, which would cost me another $150. I explained to him that the website was built on WordPress, so if you login, click on All Pages, then Add New, a new page is automatically created. You can then write whatever you want to write on the page, or copy and paste existing content. Then you click on Publish and it is done. To set the DNS, you login into your hosting account, go to Name Server and add the DNS. Then you are done. It takes less than 2 minutes to do. Sheldon had presumed that I did not know anything about website creation and operation. I paid him for the work he did and refused to pay him what he was asking me for because he had lied to me about what needed to be done. The next day, I checked my bank balance. It turned out that when I paid Sheldon for setting up my computer, the first and second payments had in fact gone through, along with the third. It was now beginning to make sense. I confronted Sheldon about charging me three times. He said it was not his fault. He explained that it was the bank's fault for providing him with a gadget that does not work. I decided to cut him off. At that point, he began to plead with me. He claimed that we were friends. Again, I was dealing with a person who professed himself a friend and then carried out a con. First Hannu and then Sheldon—I was not happy. Following this, he started calling me almost every five minutes and bombarding me with email after email. I called law enforcement and reported him. They called him and asked him to stop calling me. That was the day I made two simple decisions: 1) I would always follow my gut feeling. (Just because a person appears nice and wants to be a friend, it does not mean the person is a good person.) 2) I would not do business with anyone if I sensed that the person was desperate for money.

The Positives Out of the Negatives

Had I not worked with Mr. Walters who sent complaints about me to the company CEO causing me to be fired, my diabetes would not have been triggered and my research discoveries, self-cure, and this book would not have occurred.

When Mrs. Clarkson hired me, she told me that every cook she had hired quit on her and that she needed me to commit to the job and I agreed to this. I later found that she wanted me to commit to the job because the board of directors had begun asking why the cooks were quitting. She was using me to protect her job. The pay was not much. Had she not found a way to terminate my employment, I would still be working for her and struggling to make ends meet. Two days before she terminated my employment, I had already found work that paid me double. Was it not for the new job, I would not have had the financial means to write and publish this book on diabetes.

Because of the fraud I experienced at the hands of Hannu and his overall treatment of me, I went back to the previous web developer who had built me a professional and functional website that people said good things about. More importantly, had I not encountered Hannu, I would still be trying to promote the first version of this book that had no proof or scientific backing that type 2 diabetes can be reversed. This version has proof and endorsements. To overcome the entire traumatic experience that gave me a mild stroke and chest pain, I pulled the first version off the market, which included the cover work Hannu had done. In place of his work is the beautiful cover of this version of the book. It is exactly what I had envisioned and what Hannu had not accomplished.

As for Sheldon, after my experience with him, before agreeing to have someone work for me related to this book, I asked as many questions as necessary to ensure they were qualified to execute the particular project.

I have realized that all the people I have encountered—the bad ones, the good ones, the doctors, those who endorsed this book—plus the proof of diabetes as curable, the articles, the editor who was able to enhance what I wrote, the designer who manifested my vision of the cover, the interior designer; all of it has made this book what it is today—a fitting offering for the readers who are all an extension of the journey.

The Book with a Cure

One day, I saw an infomercial selling a book called *Natural Cures They Don't Want You to Know*. The author of the book—Kevin Trudeau—was very persuasive in the infomercial. He described the US government and drug companies as institutions hiding cures from the public, which sounded believable. Believing in natural medicine, I went ahead and ordered the book, which sold for $29.95 plus shipping. The book offered no cure. Instead, it demanded an additional $500 for a subscription to their newsletter. Through the newsletter, I would be sent the information about a cure.

Wait! It gets even worse. When I placed my order for the book, the customer service agent at the other end of the line tried to sell me a skin product telling me that if I didn't like the product, I could return it within 10 days from the purchase date for a full refund. This way, they wouldn't charge my credit card. I said to her, "But it is going to take about four weeks to receive the book and the skin product. By then, 10 business days will have passed. That means you will charge my credit card before I even receive what I bought."

The lady paused and replied, "Oh, you're right." Once again, I saw that consumers are expected to be unwitting.

The Diet Pill

Before doing my own extensive research, I did some experimentation with various products. On one occasion, after seeing an ad, I ordered some diet pills which were marketed by a man who said he was a graduate of Harvard Medical School. I was impressed by his overall presentation.

When I called to make my order, the customer service agent tried to sell me a six-month supply of the weight-loss pills along with a skin product. The main problem was that the ad said that the buyer would lose 10 pounds a month. I wanted to lose a total of 15 pounds. According to their claim of 10 pounds of weight-loss a month, I only needed enough pills for six weeks. Then the customer service agent told me that in four weeks, if I did not like the product, I should let them know so that they would not send more pills to me and not put more charges on my credit card. I asked the lady how long it would take me to receive the diet pills. She told me four weeks. I asked her, "If it takes four weeks to receive them, by then you will begin sending me more diet pills and charge my credit card before I am able to call to say I do not want the product." In this case too, the customer service agent paused for a moment before replying, "Yeah, you're right." I will say what I have already said. The sellers of these products assume that consumers don't think.

Nambudripad's Allergy Elimination Techniques (NAET)

This experience dates back to the second month after I was diagnosed with diabetes. My doctor had said that it was difficult to cure diabetes. I decided to try a service known as NAET. This would be my first try at an alternative medicine approach for reversing my diabetes. A lady I know who has faith in alternative medicine suggested that I try this technique. I didn't know anything about it nor had I heard about it previously, but by her description, it sounded interesting. According to this friend, the practitioner she recommended practiced in my area and had much experience working with diabetics. I called and made an appointment.

On my way to my first appointment, all I could think about was how I would be cured. First, the lady took my personal information and then she took my blood pressure. Next, she told me to hold onto a small transparent bottle with liquid in it. She told me she would do a reading of my body based on the temperature of my palm in order to determine what method would best suit me and indicate the direction for my cure. She also said that she was a nurse from Poland.

While I held the tiny clear bottle with the transparent liquid, she took out an L-shaped piece of metal. It was a New Age type of diving rod known as a "dowsing rod". Its other names are "vining rod" and "witching rod." As she held it near me, she explained that the device would be drawn toward the part of my body that was problematic.

After the dowsing part was over, she asked me if she could do a psychic reading with cards that sat upon the table. I consented and after her reading was complete, she said that I was a hot-tempered person. That was it for me. I was looking for a cure for my diabetes, not a tarot card reading. When she was done with the reading, she inserted needles into certain acupuncture points on my body. She left the needles there for a short time and then pulled them out while informing me that my blood sugar level would normalize. That did not happen and I did not feel better. How could she even know my blood sugar would have normalized without any blood tests? Before I left, she asked me to come back for 12 more sessions at $65 dollars each. I went home and called her to inform her that I was not interested.

Am I saying NAET does not work? It was my first time exposed to such therapy. Based on what the practitioner had done, I didn't want to continue. In addition, I had just cheated death so I was very wary about putting my health in the hands of a person who behaved like a psychic. Yes, the woman said she had been a nurse for 20 years in Poland, but she did not practice nursing in Canada even though she referred to her profession in relation to her new line of work. She also had no certificate on her office wall to indicate that she had been a nurse in Poland.

Diabetes Healing Plan

I F I MAY, HERE, I will use war as an analogy. If you go to war and are well prepared, winning becomes much easier. To approach reversing diabetes, preparation is really the key to success.

It is not uncommon for a diabetic's weight to fluctuate. It is okay to feel that, as a diabetic, you are not doing enough to improve your health. We are going to fix that. I will use my own example as a researcher because I too, at one point, felt as though I was not doing enough to improve my health.

To tackle the weight problem, I pushed myself and added five more minutes to my cardio exercise and to my surprise, by October 7, 2011, I was able to run on the treadmill for 30 minutes at a stretch. Monday, October 10th, 2011, Thanksgiving Day in Canada, I decided I had eaten too much the previous night with friends so I had to adjust my run. The next morning, for the first time, I managed to run 40 minutes at a stretch. I was so happy! To me, lasting that long was a huge accomplishment. After this adjustment to my routine, I kept checking my weight, which came down from 210 pounds and then hovered around 205 pounds. I loved it but also hated it because I was stuck at 205 pounds. However, I had a strong and undeniable feeling in my gut that I would find a cure for my diabetes. I didn't know how I was going to do it. I knew that there were no drugs out there to cure type 2 diabetes. All I knew was that I was going to cure myself of this thing. I felt that a cure was just around the corner and so, each day, I wondered if it would be today that my diabetes would be gone.

My Secret Passion

As I've mentioned, I used to indulge in all sorts of chocolate, as if chocolate was about to become extinct. As a matter of fact, in my younger days, I would tell my friends that when I died, I wanted to be buried in a coffin made of chocolate. Yes, you read correctly. I had more than just a sweet tooth—I had an ultra-sweet tooth, at the very least. If I went to the supermarket and saw one-pound boxes of chocolate truffles from France, I would buy at least six boxes. I confess—there were times when I was working as a chef that I would put chocolate mousse on the dessert menu mainly because it would be an excuse for me to indulge.

According to Dr. Robert Lustig—whom I have already quoted—and other medical doctors, sugar is toxic and is killing us. Dr. Lustig believes that sugar contributes to heart disease, diabetes, and other diseases. Sugar is linked to cancer, which thrives on sugar for growth. Sugar causes brain damage, such as Alzheimer's, and the American Heart Association is asking people to cut down on sugar consumption. Most doctors don't know how dangerous sugar is, according to Dr. Lustig. He further points out that there is data and research showing that sugar causes diabetes.

His conclusions proved that I had been right all along. I took enormous comfort in his words and so should all type 2 diabetics. The evidence is undisputable: Sugar is just as addictive as any addicting drug, such as cocaine or heroin, because sugar makes your brain produce a euphoric feeling. This feeling demands that you partake in the consumption of more sugar—more of the drug.

How much sugar should you be eating? According to Dr. Lustig, men should consume no more than 150 calories from sugar a day and women no more than 100 calories from sugar per day. He also says people should maintain a balanced diet.

3-Step Plan

There are three main components needed to heal from diabetes, which I call "steps" to make them easy to follow.

Step 1: Diet—Healthy Eating

As a trained chef, when it comes to healthy eating, I don't take advice from just anyone. There is a reason why. Put yourself in my shoes for just a moment. Years ago, I went to cooking school. The so-called diet experts claimed that we should eat more carbohydrates. Many people jumped on that bandwagon. I watched as a very beautiful female friend of mine ballooned out as a result of eating tons of pasta dishes and bread. Her weight increased so much that she had to have her stomach surgically stapled in order to lose weight. This was after liposuction failed her and the $5,000 dollars she paid was essentially thrown away.

After we devoured large amounts of carbohydrates and became fat, a new diet became popular: the "high-protein, low-carb" diet. Yet, we continued to gain weight.

The next fad was diet pills, which are nothing more than appetite suppressants. That, too, failed us miserably. Isn't it interesting that diet pills come with recipes and a recommendation that the buyer should eat healthy and exercise? This is because eating healthy in addition to exercise is the true secret to losing body fat and burning the excess sugar from your body that makes you insulin resistant. In other words, spending your money on diet pills is a complete waste of money. If the diet pills really worked, those selling them would not need to recommend the accompaniment of healthy eating and exercise. The pills should independently make you lose weight.

Proteins

Your healing plan should include protein from all the meat groups, in addition to fish and legumes. Do not cut corners by not eating a variety of protein sources. You will set yourself up for failure.

Meals and Snacks

Eat either five small meals a day or three meals and two snacks in between meals. Also, eat a final snack two hours before bed time. A type 2 diabetic must eat something every two hours. As well, you must eat within two hours of waking up or your blood sugar will drop too low, which will make you feel lightheaded.

SPECIAL NOTE: **Do not eat fruit first thing in the morning on an empty stomach!** The sugar in the fruit will spike your blood sugar level. I researched and tested eating fruits on an empty stomach, which some doctors and food scientists recommend to diabetics. Again, I do not recommend this, particularly with tropical fruits, such as:

- Pineapple
- Mango
- Banana

And any fruit that is very sweet, such as:

- Grapes
- Pears
- Honey Dew
- Cantaloupe

Recommended fruits are mostly berries, which should be eaten as dessert. Reversing diabetes depends on a very strict diet. Do it right or fail.

The Miracle Food

Beans: A wonderful protein to have with your meals. I stew mine and eat them with brown rice. Beans help balance the blood sugar level. All beans are fine. This is how I cook my beans to make them into a stew. I soak them in water overnight and then boil them until they are soft. I then strain them, put them aside, make a sauce for the stew (this can be made with tomatoes or curry) and in place of meat, add the cooked beans to the sauce. Heat the mixture for 15 few minutes and then cool it down. Is that too much work? I portion and freeze single servings for whenever I need them.

Egg Whites

If you love to have eggs for breakfast, eat egg whites. They are not just healthy but are also very high in protein with full branched-chain amino acids. The yolk is high in cholesterol so avoid it while you are on this health plan to facilitate reversing your diabetes.

Water

Drink two litres of water each day. (For American readers, this is the equivalent of 67 ounces of fluid, or slightly more than eight, eight-ounce glasses.)

NOTE: If your body is not used to lots of water, when you begin to drink more water, you will retain it in your body, but as you continue drinking larger quantities, you will begin to expel more water than previously and you will begin to lose weight. Do not panic and stop drinking water in the first week when your body is retaining it, otherwise, the previously existing weight from water will remain in your body. During my research and experimentation, the more water I drank, the more I expelled. I currently drink a minimum of four litres of water a day. I learned the hard way that I had to stop by 8 PM or I would spend all night running to the washroom.

Salads

Men, in particular, don't like salad. That includes me. But I found a way to make my salads appealing. I make half a plate of greens and top it with:

- cooked chicken breast cut up, or fish
- one egg, boiled or sliced

- walnuts
- diced cucumber
- quartered tomatoes
- berries, such as strawberries or blueberries
- any dressing.

The Perfect Carbohydrate

I had heard of quinoa but had never tried it or even known what it looked like. Diabetes research led me to discover this grain which in my view is one of the best sources of carbohydrates and protein. Quinoa apparently was considered the food of the gods in South America. Quinoa, as well as beans, is part of the group of foods known as super foods. There are two types of quinoa: the grain and the flakes. I tried the flakes at first, but they cooked out like a mush so I switched to the grain.

Cooking process for the grain: first, rinse one cup of quinoa with cold water. Place it into two cups of cold water, bring it to a boil and then cover and simmer. It has to be stirred from time to time or it will stick to the bottom of the cooking pot. Cook it until it absorbs all the liquid. It tastes great when it is cooked in vegetable or chicken stock with a little butter and salt is added for flavor. To make it really delicious, I use flavoured broth or butter, as well as dehydrated onions. The taste is out of this world. One of the most popular ways to preparae quinoa is to cook some diced onion, celery, zucchini, and red pepper in a little olive oil. Chop some parsley and toss it with the cooked vegetables and the quinoa. Right there you have a complete meal. Quinoa is now becoming very popular and can be found in the bulk section in any super market, or grocery store, as we call them in Canada.

Pasta

Many experts say that a diabetic should not eat pasta. That is not entirely true. A diabetic can eat pasta made from vegetables. The very best pasta today is kamut pasta. Kamut has something in common with quinoa; it is high in protein. Kamut has more protein than meat—pound for pound—and its protein is clean, which means; free from pesticides, heavy metals, and antibiotics. Eating cooked kamut pastas with tomato sauce and some blanched vegetables is a very tasty and healthy alternative to wheat flour pastas.

When we think about healthy eating, some of us imagine a plate full of raw foods. Healthy cooking can be fun, but it also depends on how well the meal is prepared. Healthy eating can be a turn off for many people because the food often lacks flavour or it simply tastes bad—you don't want that and I don't blame you. Many chefs have a specialty. I specialize in flavor, or food that tastes great. The kamut and quinoa meals are discoveries I made during to my diabetes research. They can taste great if they are prepared just like you would prepare any tasty dish. Some food scientists, such as Dr. Fuhrman, are advocates of a strict vegan diet. In March of 2013, an insurance executive whose wife is diabetic was telling me that he finds the diet in Dr. Fuhrman's recipe book for diabetics too strict and thinks that it will fail people. When a diet is too strict, people are likely to cheat. If you are diabetic you can eat tasty food that is healthy and still self-cure yourself. For example, if you like pasta with tomato sauce, vegetables, and tuna, you can use a recipe that I have cooked hundreds of times in restaurants—just replace the white pasta with a vegetable or kamut pasta.

I consulted with a naturopathic doctor and learned that a diabetic's cholesterol level can go up rather quickly. This is mainly due to a diabetic's body not being able to absorb maximum nutrition from the food they eat. This is why eating healthy is so important.

Portion Sizes

What size portion should you eat? This is what was recommended to me:

- **Cooked Protein**

    Fowl—palm size

    Veggie protein—palm size

    Fish—palm size

- **Cooked Carbohydrate**

    Steel-cut oatmeal—size of a fist

    Brown rice—size of a fist

    Quinoa—size of a fist

- **Fat**

    Add one teaspoon of olive oil to salads and add one tablespoon cream to steal-cut oatmeal to help with digestion.

Sweetener

There are all sorts of sweeteners on the market today, many claimed to be perfect for diabetics. Use stevia or agave and nothing else. Stevia is derived from a plant leaf. It comes in a transparent liquid or powder form and can be used in tea or coffee.

Because of the things that I have gone through and what life has taught me, I have taken control of my own life and you should do the same. For example, many people claim that soft drinks do not contribute to diabetes, yet diabetics are often asked to keep a can of soda with them just in case their blood sugar level drops too low. Most of these drinks can raise the blood sugar level within 11 seconds. Some of these drinks contain up to 65 grams of sugar in a can and up to 90 grams in a "Big Gulp." This information is readily available online. If a soft drink raises the blood sugar level in a diabetic, would it not do the same to a non-diabetic, and if it does, what does that mean? As my doctor said, reversing type 2 diabetes takes nothing more than common sense.

Foods Diabetics Must NOT Indulge In

Foods a diabetic must never indulge in are foods that add pounds to one's weight. Shedding one's extra pounds will help the diabetic's chance of reversing his or her condition during the diabetes-reversal process. Many foods that cause weight-gain are fatty, hence; they increase cholesterol levels. If you are diabetic and love such foods, don't lose hope. The human body is so perfectly made that it heals itself. It can process any food that is put into it and the liver filters out toxins, but for it to do its work the way it is designed to it has to be given proper care. There is a saying you may already be familiar with, which is "garbage in, garbage out." Put dirty oil in your car and it will break down. Feed your body garbage and it will break down. Once a diabetic heals from diabetes, the person can reintroduce less healthy foods into his or her diet, in moderation, and this includes even soft drinks. The key is moderation. For example, I had a burger for dinner that I made for clients at work. It was the first burger I had this year and I put homemade tartar sauce on it instead of mayonnaise. On top, I also put a slice of Swiss cheese, some bacon, tomato, lettuce, and a slice of pickle. That is what I mean by moderation. So far this year, I have not had more than one litre of my favourite soda. I usually top up the soda with half a glass of milk. The body can handle that much soda because it is not being overwhelmed. Now that I have cured my diabetes, I have these moderate indulgences. While in the reversal process, I did not eat and would not recommend that you eat these foods:

- Burgers with all the trimmings
- Pizza
- High-calorie sandwiches
- Any type of white rice
- Cooked Chinese food from the supermarket
- Large portions of any meal during each week
- Candy bars
- Ice cream
- White pasta with meat sauce
- Fried meats

If you are a type 2 diabetic endeavouring to reverse your diabetes by doing as I have so far indicated, you are on your way to reversing your condition in a month or less (as I did as a result of my research and experimentation).

In a research study that is being conducted by UK Diabetes, they have reported that it took their participants four months to reverse their diabetes with a success rate of 40%. My own reversal took 21 days and this is because I took the steps of which I am now giving an overview. These include a specific menu cycle, an exercise routine, as well as vitamin therapy.

Step 2: Exercise

I receive emails from diabetics who express some frustration over the fact that they have followed their doctor's advice to exercise, but have seen no improvement in their condition. There is a reason why this happens. There are specific ways the exercises should be executed, including cardiovascular ones and use of exercise machines. Researchers in the field of kinesiology have discovered that though lifting free weights helps build bigger muscles and makes you stronger, if you stop going to the gym, you quickly lose that muscle strength and the muscle will eventually turn into fat. On the other hand, resistance training makes you stronger and firms and tones your body more effectively. With resistance training, even if you stop going to the gym for a month or two, you will retain almost all your muscle strength. I recommend that the diabetic use resistance exercise machines as much as possible.

Remember that diabetes affects the muscles by making them weak, so the diabetic needs to make the muscles stronger. The manner in which the muscles are worked during the exercise routine needs to be considered. According to my testing, resistance training, or working with resistance machines in the gym is best for diabetics. One of the things I like the most about resistance machines is that since they resist, the particular muscles that are being worked on are forced to work harder. Adding to the benefit of the resistance machines is the fact that the chance of injury is kept to a minimum.

Cardiovascular Exercise

Through my research I leaned that many sports experts advocate running. I tried this, but it was not for me. I went to see a Chinese medicine practitioner who told me that while jogging was good, in order to see substantial results, I needed to increase my effort during exercise to the point where I broke into a sweat and sustained that condition for a certain amount of time. I am pleased that Dr. Xiao Qin provided me with this key advice.

Note on Going to the Gym

If you are a diabetic and are not used to going to the gym, please consult with a physician before you start. I will relate a real-life experience to explain why.

I met a heavyset man who was diabetic. He was new at the gym we both belonged to. The man was in his late 50s. In his first few days at the gym, he really pushed himself. He would sit on a stationary bike and peddle for 30 minutes while he struggled to get his breath. His wife took notice and asked him to go slowly, but he would not listen. Suddenly, during one of his struggles for breath, he collapsed and never regained consciousness. He died. According to his wife, he overdid his exercise and died from a heart attack. His demise was very unfortunate.

My advice to you is that as a diabetic, before you undertake any exercise, talk to your doctor and ask what type of exercise you should do and how much you should do in the beginning. I also strongly warn that you should be aware of your body and not put strain on it. Build up your strength gradually.

Benefits of Exercise

According to the *New York Times*, two thirds of Americans are overweight, fat, or obese. There are a number of benefits to exercising rather than taking appetite suppressants or diet pills.

Exercise does the following:

- reduces cholesterol

- helps in maintaining good health and developing new good habits

- makes you far more spiritually "in tune" by clearing your mind

- makes you feel good and rejuvenated

- strengthens your heart, muscles, and even bones.

I have mentioned my dermatologist, Dr. Allan, who said that if people would exercise and eat moderately, 90% of their ailments would disappear. The most important thing about exercising to help reverse type 2 diabetes is defined by the researchers in Europe who found that exercise is only effective when a routine is followed. Does it make sense to you to exercise without results?

Step 3: Vitamin and Supplement Therapy

The last part of the healing plan for reversing type 2 diabetes is vitamin and supplement therapy. The more I researched, the more I learned about the need for supplements (supplements include vitamins, minerals, amino acids, herbs, and botanicals) in a complete diabetes reversal plan.

You may be wondering why a type 2 diabetic would necessarily include supplements. Consider this: When I was diagnosed diabetic, I realized the damage the sugar buildup had done to my body. Like other newly diagnosed diabetics, my body was not absorbing enough nutrients from the food I consumed. This is why one of the suggestions made to a diabetic when he or she is sent to a diabetes clinic to learn how to manage the diabetes is to take vitamins. A diabetic body does not function normally. It is a simple fact. In my case, the first thing the pharmacist (the one who works with diabetics and who advised me) recommended was that I start taking supplements right away. Once I researched and learned more about how a diabetic's body functions, his advice made perfect sense to me.

He also strongly recommended that I begin cooking my own food. "Processed foods are out of the question," the pharmacist informed me. Cooking one's own food allows the diabetic to have complete control of how the meal is prepared and what he or she puts into the stomach. I was very fortunate to have been introduced to someone who knew a lot about diabetes and told me, upfront, that type 2 diabetes can be cured. His words gave me hope and I hope reading this book gives you hope.

Super Multivitamin

I have mentioned already that a diabetic's body does not adequately assimilate nutrition from the intake of food. Therefore, it is imperative for vitamins to be introduced into the diabetic's diet. In my particular case, because of the damage diabetes had inflicted on my body and the advancement of my condition, I started my vitamin therapy by taking two super vitamins a day so that there would be a buildup of nutrients in my body.

I reduced the vitamin to the normal, daily dosage after the first month.

Calcium

Calcium assists with building strong bones. There are those who say that male adults over the age of 40 must not drink milk or take calcium because it could lead to kidney stones. That is true. I checked with my doctor. However, as a diabetic, my body was not absorbing this much-needed nutrient and I did temporarily need the supplement as part of my healing plan.

Chromium

This supplement was recommended to me by a naturopath. The purpose of this mineral is to help the body metabolize sugar.

Omega 3 Super Concentrate

It was the pharmacist who specializes in working with diabetics who told me that Omega 3 works to protect the heart. Now consider this secondary reason and you be the judge of the need for this supplement: When I was diagnosed, my doctor asked that I take a test to see if any damage had been done to my heart by the high level of sugar in my body. In addition, when I was sent to the diabetes clinic to learn how to manage the diabetes, I was told that eventually, I would have a heart condition. In other words, because of the diabetes, ultimately, I would develop heart disease. The test my doctor recommended in addition to what the nurse at the diabetes clinic said about heart disease supported my taking Omega 3. I am grateful that the pharmacist recommended it to me.

Vitamin D3

When it comes to this particular vitamin, Blacks have no option but to take it for two reasons:

1. Blacks who live in countries where the seasons include winter do not produce their own vitamin D.

2. Vitamin D3 is called the "sun vitamin" because, when we expose ourselves to sunlight, the body produces vitamin D for itself.

Fenugreek

Some doctors who specialize in nutrition science state that fenugreek is helpful in controlling blood sugar. I tried it, but soon noticed that it had a strong fragrance which emanated from my skin. I could smell it on my cloths and on my bed sheets. Despite the smell caused by the fenugreek, I was on a mission to achieve my objective and this overrode the consideration of body odour.

Other Supplements to Consider

- Gymnema Sylvestre
- Zinc
- Probiotics

I used the above supplements in specific dosages and at specific times of the day. While I was on vitamin therapy, my doctor kept me on prescription drugs. I am not suggesting that type 2 diabetics run out and purchase all the supplements I have recommended. There is risk associated with taking supplements incorrectly. At the end of this book, I will provide specific information on what type 2 diabetics interested in reversing their diabetes can do.

Don't Let Diabetes Defeat You

My journey afforded me the opportunity to speak with people involved in the same field of research. A common thread throughout their view of diabetics was that rather than take action to heal themselves, diabetics give in to the condition with excuses, such as, "Only 300 pills cost $60 dollars," or, "I can't keep up the exercise and diet." Easily defeated, they decide it is okay to just manage the diabetes.

This type of diabetic is the kind product manufacturers love. To boost their business, a leading physiatrist is employed by drug companies to classify conditions as diseases. Such an example is the classifying of anxiety as a disease. When something is classified as a disease, new drugs can be manufactured for the so-called disease. Such practices were partly the basis of a report from The University of British Columbia accusing drug manufacturers of selling drugs to people when they are not needed.

There are often two sides to any particular scientific perspective. With the topic at hand, science shows that diabetes drugs are of benefit, but they also cause damage. Another disturbing fact is that some diabetes drugs have been pulled off the market yet are still sold on the Internet.

Settling for taking drugs instead of adopting a natural-cure plan for healing from a reversible condition is in my view, defeatism. This defeatism will allow type 2 diabetes to progress to type 1 and kill the patient. Along this road of degeneration, the diabetes will trigger many other diseases, which I have already identified in this book.

Acupuncture

I am not the type of person who likes to see needles going into my body. I have been like that as far back as I can recall. So you can imagine how I felt about doing a daily blood sugar test by pricking my finger tips to draw blood after meals each day. As part of my healing plan, I decided to add acupuncture, (more needles)—a decision I made after learning about its benefits through my research. Practitioners say that acupuncture (which is a part of Asian medicine, not just Chinese, as it is also practiced in Korean medicine,) works by stimulating the body so that it corrects itself.

Reversing type 2 diabetes is best when several approaches are used together, as advised by my doctor. I was able to reverse my diabetes in less than a month mainly because I created a comprehensive healing plan for reviving my body's insulin sensitivity. This successful plan was developed through research and experimentation. The result was that the diabetes was reversed in less than a month.

In the beginning, I was highly skeptical that type 2 diabetes could be reversed, especially in my severe case. That was one of the reasons why I managed my diabetes for a while. After my doctor definitively told me that diabetes type 2 could be reversed and cured, I consulted with other doctors for more opinions. When I learned that acupuncture could help, before incorporating it into my healing plan, I contacted the acupuncture school and asked if diabetes could be cured, in their opinion. I did not ask if acupuncture itself could reverse or cure diabetes. The answer I received was "Yes, but there is a condition." The condition was that I MUST take all sugar out of my diet. When I say sugar, I don't just mean white sugar. This includes honey and other sweeteners—but not stevia.

Acupuncture does not cure diabetes. It is an optional treatment which can be used to help the body heal itself. Similarly, a healing plan does not reverse type 2 diabetes; what it does is give the body what it needs to reverse the diabetes and heal itself. It is like I said earlier about putting dirty oil in your car engine versus putting in clean oil and the results of both. The human body is well engineered in that it heals itself if you give it the healthy things it needs. If a headache medicine is taken, it does not heal the body—it blocks the pain but does not help the body to remove or heal the cause of the pain.

The purpose of my healing plan is to give the diabetic body what it needs to rapidly heal itself. The research done before the writing of this book was independent and self-funded.

There is a large research project going on in the UK, the basic principles of which have been included in this book. That research supports the principle that if the body is given what it needs, it can heal itself from diabetes. Their focus is diet and exercise, and most importantly, a *customized* diet and exercise plan. More than two years ago, my research resulted in the same conclusion and methods. Furthermore, the success rate for the system found in this book has been much higher than the UK study's because it goes beyond just diet and exercise by including vitamin therapy along with other supplements, such as probiotics. Probiotics have been shown to prevent the re-occurrence of diabetes once it is reversed.

Questions and Answers

Q. DOES SUGAR CAUSE type 2 diabetes?

A. Sugar is the main cause of type 2 diabetes. On August 5, 2012, the show *60 Minutes* did a feature on research being conducted on sugar's effects on our health. It was discovered that sugar causes these three conditions and diseases:

- Hypertension
- Heart disease
- Type 2 diabetes

One expert who has become a crusader to end the excessive consumption of sugar is Dr. Lustig. According to Dr. Lustig and many like him, refined sugar is killing us. He also says that sugar causes diabetes.

Corn syrup and high-fructose corn syrup are used in many processed foods. Our body breaks sugar down into fructose and glucose, so corn syrup and sugar end up with the same chemical structure. It is only the liver that can metabolize significant amounts of fructose. When the liver cannot assimilate all the fructose derived from sugar or from corn syrup, it turns the fructose into fat. Some of that fat can get trapped in the liver. High fructose consumption is also associated with insulin resistance, obesity, and type 2 diabetes, to name a few outcomes.

Other research has found that glucose is food for cancer tumors and causes cancer to grow. Some medical doctors go as far as to advise that we should not eat sugar at all. Sugar causes pleasure and it is addicting. So can sugar be consumed safely? The answer is yes. For men, it is advisable to consume no more than 150 calories from sugar per day and for women, 100 calories from sugar per day.

Q. How do I know when my type 2 diabetes is reversed?

A. When you have reversed your diabetes type 2 using the reversal plan recommended in this book, you will begin to feel a surge of energy which peaks after about three days. This means that your body has again become insulin sensitive; in other words, you are no longer diabetic. You should also feel much healthier and stronger. More importantly, once you feel this energy surge, see your doctor for a new blood glucose test for confirmation that you are no longer diabetic.

Q. Do supplements really help in curing diabetes?

A. Yes. When you are diagnosed, often you are sent to a diabetes clinic to learn how to manage the condition. The reason why the nurses or your doctor make the suggestion to take vitamins is that when you become diabetic, your body does not absorb and process enough nutrients found in the food you eat. Thus, vitamin therapy is very important.

Q. After type 2 diabetes is reversed, can you return to being diabetic?

A. The answer is yes—if you return to the same lifestyle that made you a diabetic in the first place. Another way to look at it is, if a person likes to sit in the sun without protection and then develops skin cancer, physicians may be able to remove the cancer. However, if the person goes back to sitting in the sun for the same amount of time it took to acquire the skin cancer, that person may acquire skin cancer again.

Q. Can my blood sugar become elevated after reversing my diabetes and does that mean I have become diabetic again?

A. To answer this question for myself, I did an experiment.

The Experiment

I wanted to know that if my blood sugar became elevated, would that mean I had become diabetic again? For one month—all of May 2012—I went back to the same lifestyle I used to live. I recall going to the store and buying a certain brand of chocolate and mint milk. It was like drinking sugary mint syrup. I drank it when my friend and I were on a camping trip and it made me feel sick. Still, I ate candy bars each day, not to mention the rest of the same bad foods that had caused my diabetes. Then, at the end of the month, I did a blood test. The results are below. You can clearly see that my blood sugar level was elevated.

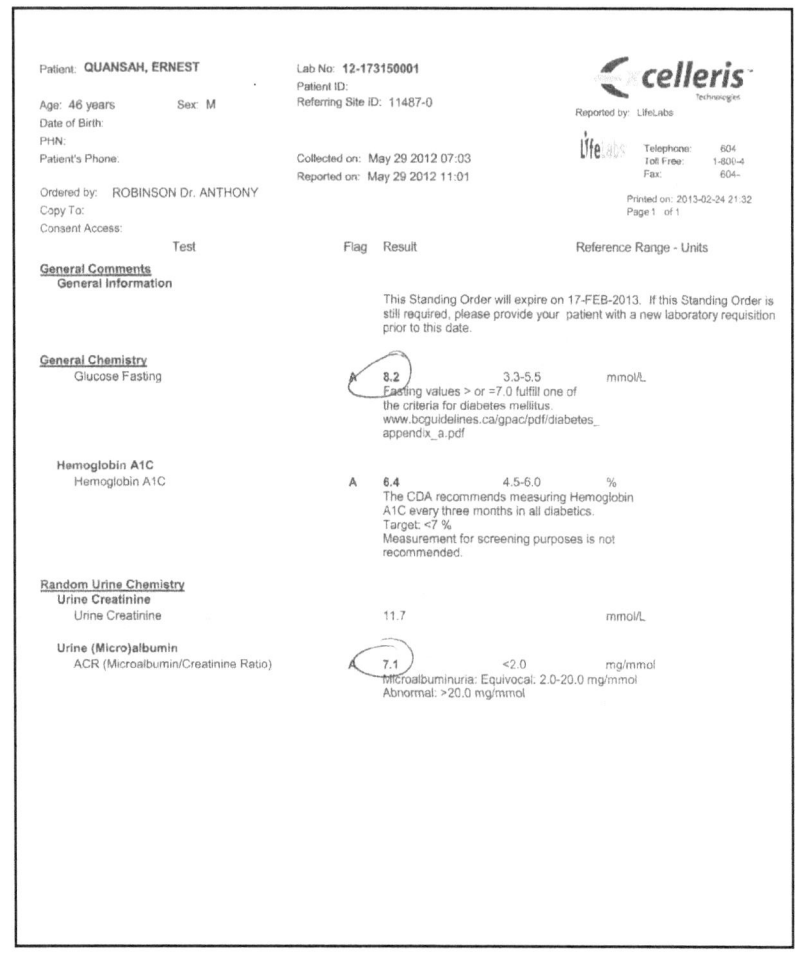

The experiment: blood test results showing blood sugar elevation.

Does this mean I had become diabetic again and within only one month? Blood sugar elevation is actually common. It occurs when you consume too much sugar. It does not mean that the person has become diabetic, though it serves as a warning about the choices the person is making and what can happen. After one month, I ended the experiment and my blood glucose level returned to normal.

Q. How long should it take before a diabetic can expect restored insulin sensitivity?

A. It depends on how well the diabetic commits to the self-cure program.

Q. Can the healing plan help people who are pre-diabetic avoid becoming full-blown diabetics?

A. The healing plan talked about in my book and offered in full detail from my website is absolutely perfect for helping pre-diabetics avoid becoming full-blown diabetics, if it is followed diligently.

Q. What defines the cure of diabetes?

A. When diabetes is reversed and the diabetic sustains the new lifestyle, and after two years the diabetes has not returned, the diabetic is considered cured, according the physician who assisted me with my research.

Q. Can a diabetic drink alcohol?

A. I don't know how alcohol impacts diabetics. What I do know is that a report came from the U.K. saying that 40% of cancer cases are caused by consumption of alcohol. For a diabetic, limiting or omitting alcohol is really common sense. If it contributes 40% to cancer in non-diabetics, imagine what it will do to diabetics, considering the body is not able to process things well when one is diabetic.

Q. Can a diabetic smoke?

A. The answer is no. I spoke to my family doctor about this same topic. He warns against smoking if you are diabetic. As we know, smoking is the number one cause of lung cancer. Smoking is a form of slow suicide that people choose to inflict upon themselves. If you know that a substance or a food item can kill you or make you ill but you choose to indulge anyway, you are accountable for making that choice. Damage done by smoking cannot be reversed.

Q. When should I eat my last meal while reversing my condition?

A. The best time to eat your last meal of the day is one hour before bed; preferably something very light.

Q. What is the best meal a diabetic should eat at night and at what time?

A. A diabetic should eat light. A small vegetable platter with hummus is what I eat two hours before bedtime.

Q. How many meals should I eat a day?

A. A diabetic should eat about five small meals a day and, if possible, eat every two to two and a half hours. After three hours of not eating, the liver will begin to produce sugar. This should be avoided by eating on time.

Q. What should a diabetic do when he or she is following the doctor's advice but is not able to reverse the diabetes?

A. The diabetic should look at his or her meal and exercise plan. Is the person cheating? Is the person going to the gym randomly and doing random exercise? Is the person eating at random? Failing to impose self-discipline and adhere to a customized menu cycle and exercise routine like the 3-Step Program I created will result in the diabetes not being reversed.

Q. What should one do when one feels hungry one hour after eating?

A. When a person feels hungry or gets a burning feeling in the stomach shortly after eating, he or she should not eat then because that feeling of hunger is actually the body burning the belly fat. The person should wait and the feeling will dissipate.

Q. Should a diabetic eat cheese while on the 3-Step Program for diabetes reversal?

A. Some dieticians suggest eating cheese for protein content. Cheese is fatty, even the so-called nonfat cheese. Cheese can increase the cholesterol level and it is not recommended that diabetics trying to reverse their diabetes eat cheese.

Q. Can an overweight or obese person who is not diabetic benefit from using the 3-Step Program offered through your website?

A. Absolutely. The 3-Step Program can help overweight and obese people lose weight very rapidly—up to 10 pounds a month—which is the average maximum weight a person can lose each month.

Q. What sort of exercise should I do?

A. The best exercise for a type 2 diabetic is resistance training.

Q. How often should I exercise to reverse my diabetes?

A. The 3-Step Program answers this question best.

Q. How long should I work out with weights each day?

A. For about one hour. Make sure to warm up on the treadmill for five minutes. When you begin with the weights, don't take more than one and a half minutes of rest in between reps. Doing this will make you sweat, which is very helpful in the reversal process.

Q. I have been exercising. I lost weight for about two weeks. Then it stopped and my weight has remained the same. Why is that?

A. Two things could be happening: 1) Your body has gotten used to the cardio and has stopped burning fat. To remedy that, add more time to your cardio exercise and make sure to bring the rate of your heartbeat to between 150 and 160. 2) The other possibility is that you have been doing intense cardio and your body is beginning to replace the fat with muscle. Muscle weighs more than fat so this will make you feel you are not progressing. The best thing to do is have the gym test your body fat on a weekly basis. When the body fat is gone, you will look thinner but your weight might be the same.

Q. What cardio machine is best for diabetes reversal?

A. My preference is the elliptical machine, and my second is the treadmill. When you use the treadmill, remember to challenge yourself. On days when you feel that you only want to walk, to speed up your heart rate, put the treadmill on a slight incline and use a walking speed. The best cardio machine, again, in my opinion, is the elliptical machine.

Q. Can using interactive video games for my exercise help?

A. No, using interactive video games is not recommended. You must use weights to help your muscles improve your insulin sensitivity. You also must do the proper cardio that will allow you to break a sweat and keep your heart beating at a good pace. That is what helps melt the fat away, leading to complete reversal of type 2 diabetes.

Q. Does exercise have other benefits?

A. The answer is yes. Knowledge abounds. Many food scientists believe that exercising three to four times a week—not more than one hour with weights—eating healthy foods, taking fish oil, vitamin D, and a high quality multivitamin improves brain health, slows down the aging process, prevents or slows down Alzheimer's, lowers cholesterol, reduces the risk of heart disease, and helps you maintain a healthy weight. There is no reason why anyone should be diabetic or die of heart disease when there is so much information available on how to avoid these eventualities.

Q. After a late session of exercise, when should I take my vitamins?

A. You can do 15 to 20 minutes of light cardio up to an hour before bedtime. You will sleep well. Don't do vigorous exercise too close to your bedtime—you will not fall asleep. If you take vitamins before bedtime, you will stay up all night. I tell you this from experience. So, don't take your vitamins at night.

Q. From where can I buy safe, good supplements?

A. The first thing you MUST understand about purchasing supplements is that they are not tested or regulated. Anyone can set up a supplement store and make unfounded claims. Some supplements have ingredients in them that can cause liver failure and even heart attacks. When you buy your supplements, ask if the ingredients in the product have been tested and which lab did the testing. Your best bet is to buy supplements made by a reputable company. There are some food scientists who have teamed up with labs to develop supplements. Their supplements are a little more expensive but you know you are spending your money on good products. All I can say is *buyer beware*.

Q. Can I take other supplements besides the ones you recommend in your program?

A. I can only recommend the supplements I used because I know they work. If you wish to add others, consult with your doctor first.

Q. When is a good time to take probiotics?

A. Probiotics should be taken in the morning, before breakfast on an empty stomach. In the morning, there is less acid in your stomach to destroy the good bacteria and this will allow the probiotics to reach your stomach and colonize. You want to take probiotic tablets with an enteric coating. You only need to take them once a day.

Q. Should I continue to take supplements after the insulin sensitivity is restored?

A. For good measure, I continue to take a multivitamin, one tablet of calcium, and one tablet of vitamin D3 in the morning with my first meal, and then take the same without the multivitamin with dinner.

Q. Can the supplements alone reverse type 2 diabetes?

A. No, they will not. No supplement, including cinnamon, can reverse type 2 diabetes. The best way to reverse type 2 diabetes, (according to all the experts including my own family doctor,) is to exercise, take your supplements, and take sugar out of your diet. All three steps must be combined in order to reverse your diabetes.

Q. My brain needs sugar for fuel. If I take refined sugar and starch out of my diet, how can I feed my brain?

A. There is enough sugar in green vegetables to supply your brain with the sugar it requires. In total, your whole body needs no more than one teaspoon of sugar in your blood. If the body is overwhelmed with sugar, it causes the pancreas to shut down and not be able to secrete enough insulin to counteract the sugar. So remember, you can get your sugar from eating enough vegetables. If you exercise, I recommend adding quinoa, kamut pasta, and other good carbohydrates to your meals, unless you want to lose weight. Then I would suggest taking out grains that provide you with carbohydrates until you achieve your ideal weight. That is what I did.

Q. Can I take diet pills to help me lose body fat while I am on this program?

A. Diet pills are an absolute no-no. I don't recommend diet pills of any kind.

Q. I have been taking probiotics. Are there foods or any drugs that might kill off the probiotics in my gut?

A. The answer is YES. Here are the top three things that can kill good bacteria:

1. *Antibiotics.* The word "anti" means against. When you are given an antibiotic by your doctor, it does what it is supposed to do. However, antibiotics do not discriminate and will also kill off the good bacteria (probiotics) in your gut.

2. *Chlorinated water.* Tap water has chlorine in it to kill harmful bacteria before you drink it. The problem is that when you drink tap water, it still has chlorine in it. Chlorine, also, does

not discriminate and will kill the good and bad bacteria in your gut. Boil your tap water; let it cool before you drink it. I also recommend using a filter that removes the chlorine.

3. *Sugar.* Last on the top-three list of probiotics killers is sugar. Sugar is fuel for bad bacteria. When bad bacteria feeds on sugar, they increase in your gut. When they increase, they kill the good bacteria. In addition, sugar helps promote infections. When I say sugar, I am referring to table sugar, including brown sugar. Brown sugar is nothing more than white refined sugar with molasses added to it. It is no healthier for you than refined white sugar. Refined sugars are found in candy bars, cookies, donuts, and processed foods.

Q. Should I take muscle-building supplements during my post-diabetes exercise routine to help rebuild my muscles?

A. The answer is no. According to the FDA, most diet supplements don't work and this includes body-building supplements. There are very few body-building supplements that can help you build muscle. The rest are all fraudulently presented. Don't be fooled by some muscular guy you saw on a bodybuilding website.

Q. What causes diabetes?

A. I have discussed some of the causes. However, it might benefit you to know that on June 29th, 2012, *Global BC News Hour* reported that a US researcher discovered that junk food causes the human body to become insulin resistant. In addition to this, the researcher rated junk food as worse than fatty foods. What is "junk food?" Candy bars, chips, cookies, doughnuts, sugar-filled snacks, and soft drinks. One cannot dispute the truth in respect to what causes diabetes any longer.

Q. Is drinking tap water good for diabetics?

A. There is a reason why, as one who was type 2 diabetic, I choose not to drink water right out of the tap. According to Monica Emelko, a professor of Environmental Engineering at Waterloo University and guest on CTV on September 22, 2014, our tap water is not as safe as we are led to believe. She has discovered that our drinking water contains pharmaceuticals, paint thinner, and a number of other toxic chemicals. There is an instance when drinking water found its way into certain streams with fish in them and some of the male fish in those streams developed female genital organs. This change in sexual organs with fish and other water creatures has been going on for a number of years and is well documented by scientists, such as Dr. David Suzuki and others.

In my view, a type 2 diabetic should not and must not drink water straight out of the tap. Your body is not as healthy as that of a non-diabetic. I would also not recommend purchasing bottled water, especially when you do not recycle the empty plastic bottle. I use a water jug that takes a replaceable filter that filters out chlorine and heavy metals from tap water. I keep the jug of water in my fridge so that it stays fresh and cool. The filter should be changed every two to three months.

Q. What are other causes of diabetes?

A. In May of 2012, *PBS Evening News* reported that the US government discovered that type 2 diabetes is often caused by:

- Bad diet
- Smoking
- Lack of exercise

★★★

Good luck reversing and curing your type 2 diabetes. Remember this piece of advice from me: Type 2 diabetes, according to the medical community, is most common in Blacks in North America, followed by Whites, Hispanics, and then Asians. If, as a Black man, I was able to reverse my diabetes in 21 days—cure it—and even rebuild my body from fat to lean muscle, there is no reason why everyone with type 2 diabetes cannot do the same. And may I remind you that when I was diagnosed, the level of sugar in my body was so high that it had begun to exit through my tongue and out of the corners of my eyelids. Worst of all, in Canada the highest level a type 2 diabetic normally reaches before going into coma followed by death is 30 millimoles. My blood sugar level was at 21. If I was able to cheat death and return to health, I see no reason why you can't.

Self-Cure Resources

(available through the Discover Diabetes Self-Cure website)

7-day Menu Plan: Special foods to eat that will also keep your weight down permanently.

Supplements Plan: The supplements I took, at what time of day, and the reason why they needed to be taken in a certain sequence to be effective.

Exercise Program: An explanation of what exercises to do and how to perform them properly in such a way that you will see results.

Slowing Down the Aging Process: Learn the natural way of living in order to live a long life, and feel young, vibrant, and as healthy as possible.

Look Fit and Feel Great: I included tips on how to lose weight as a diabetic—something that most diabetics struggle with.

Post-diabetes Body Restoration: Type 2 diabetes turns your muscle into fat. Learn how to restore your muscles after you have self-cured your diabetes.

✸✸✸

Food Trap

If you are a type 2 diabetic and have not taken anything else from this book, take this piece of advice: If you are trying to self-cure your type 2 diabetes, watch out for the "food trap." It is very much akin to a monkey trap. A monkey trap is set with a nice, tasty banana dangling behind a small hole in a container that cannot be moved. The hole is just large enough for the monkey to insert its hand to grab the banana. The problem is that once the monkey grabs onto the banana, its closed fist is too big for the monkey to pull the banana out through the hole. The monkey then has two choices:

1. It can let go of the banana, pull its hand out, and find freedom.

2. It can hang onto the banana and be caught by the trapper who will do with the monkey as he wishes.

The food trap is no different. If diabetics insist on eating refined sugar, soft drinks, donuts, candy bars, sweet desserts, and junk foods, (which the United States government has reported to be the very worst food—worse than fatty foods and responsible for causing obesity and inflammation, and promoting diabetes,) their lives will be at the hands of companies that make these foods. If you are diabetic and *you* don't care about what these sweetened products are doing to you, will anyone else? If you let go of these foods and follow the program that I have made available on my website, you will be freed from the grip of the food that is killing you.

THAT, TO ME, IS REAL FREEDOM.

How Type 2 Diabetes Can Be Reversed and Cured

IN APRIL 2017, I prepared a video presentation for the International Diabetes and Degenerative Disease conference. The conference is hosted and organized by Clyto Access and will take place on September 14 and 15 of 2017. This entire chapter is the uncut written version of my presentation, which I feel makes a nice summational final chapter for the book.

One or more statements made in this presentation may be found in previous chapters. The intention of the repetition is to stress the importance of certain facts that should not to be taken casually by diabetics.

Presentation for the International Diabetes and Degenerative Disease Conference

Ernest Quansah (Presenter)
Type 2 Diabetes Researcher and Educator

Topic: Research on How to Reverse Your Diabetes

- My research and area of expertise is type 2 diabetes and how it is reversed.

- In 2012, 1.5 million people died worldwide as a result of diabetes. These deaths were preventable.

- Each day that diabetics do nothing about their condition, their chances of blindness, leg amputation, stroke, and heart disease increase—but all this is preventable.

- In Canada, the government spends $23 billion on diabetes each year. In the United States, the figure is estimated to be over $245 billion a year.

- In the UK, the number of diabetics has risen from 700,000 in the 1990s to 2.8 million today.

- Experts in this field say that if diabetes is not brought under control, by the year 2040, 1 out of every 8 people will be diabetic: a staggering 1.8 billion people worldwide.

- There is mounting evidence and research that shows that type 2 diabetes can be reversed.

Signs of oncoming diabetes:

- Craving for sweets
- Frequent urination
- Rapid weight loss
- Tingling at the finger tips and toes

In 2009, I was diagnosed a diabetic. I awoke each morning to find a sticky, whitish substance on my tongue as well as in the corners of my eyes. I made a visit to the doctor. After asking me a few questions, he ordered a blood glucose text. That same afternoon, his receptionist summoned me back to his office.

Tests showed a blood glucose level of 21.9 millimoles per litre or 394.6 milligrams, more than five times the normal levels of 4.0 to 6.5 mmol/L.

My doctor informed me that I was steps away from going into cardiac arrest. He further explained that the sticky, whitish substance on my tongue and in the corners of my eyes each morning was the sugar that had built up in my body and was trying to find a way to exit my body.

On the next page you can see my blood test result when I was diagnosed a diabetic.

I managed the diabetes for a while just like most diabetics. One day, I was doing random research on diabetes when I came across a video by Dr. Fuhrman. In his video, according to him, drug companies came to him with a proposal to write an article on diabetes. When he completed the article, the drug companies refused to publish the article saying that if they published the article, diabetics would know that they can reverse their diabetes. When I came across this information, I was floored. But it was about to get better.

I watched a video of a conference in which a prominent, white South African physician stated that cancer can be cured. At that point, I felt as though he was talking to me telling me to conduct research and learn how I can cure my diabetes. I could not believe what I had stumbled across.

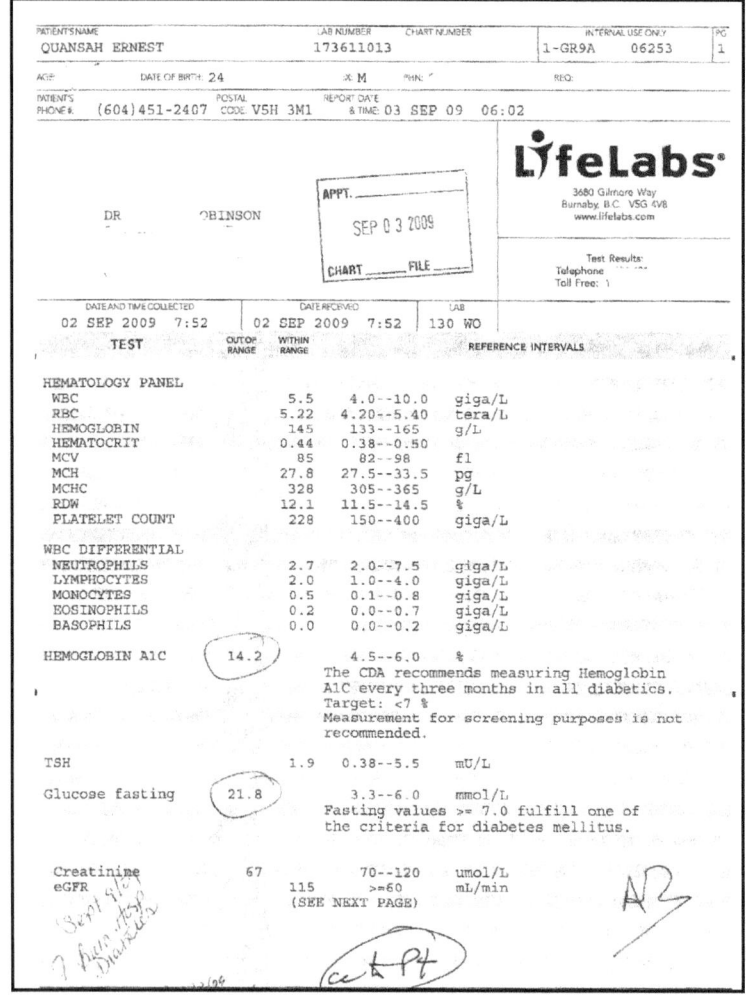

My blood test result when I was diagnosed a diabetic.

What happened next confirmed to me that I must act, for without acting, how would I know if I could be cured or not. I was watching one of my favourite shows titled *The Nature of Things* hosted by a local scientist, David Suzuki. The episode explored why so many obese and overweight people have tried and tried but could not lose weight.

One of the researchers featured on the show that day was Dr. Paula Baillie-Hamilton, Ph.D. and professor at Oxford University, who was not able to lose the extra weight she had gained during pregnancy. Her scientific research showed the reason she could not lose weight was something called obesogens. **Obesogens** are chemical compounds found in the red meat we eat that disrupt normal development and balance of lipid metabolism, which in some cases, can lead to obesity. This happens when the chemicals program the individual's genes to produce fat. So as the overweight or obese person loses weight, the weight comes right back. For years, people eat red meat that is making them fat. What I learned aligned with what I knew about how processed foods are intentionally designed to addict the consumer so that he or she eats even more of the same food that is not healthy for them. This predicament reminded me of my younger years when I was a smoker. I had an enormously difficult time quitting because the cigarette had the addicting substance, nicotine, aside from other harmful, poisonous chemicals compounds found in cigarettes. It was all becoming very clear to me. Foods we are supposed to enjoy are harmful to us but to make it worse, the foods are designed to make the consumer become addicted to them. This discovery gave me a WOW reaction. I was shocked.

Dr. Baillie-Hamilton (after her research on why she was having problems losing weight) authored *Toxic Overload* to help other mothers and perhaps people struggling to lose weight understand the underlying cause of their failure to shed off the pounds. I was greatly excited by her book. I said previously—information is power.

Inspired by Dr. Baillie-Hamilton's approach, the first step I took was to make an appointment with my doctor. At the appointment I asked him point blank: "Dr. Robinson, can type 2 diabetes be cured?" He replied, "Yes." I sought out a second and third opinion and sure enough, all the other doctors confirmed what my doctor had told me. I undertook my own research to find a way to defeat my diabetes. I wanted to see if diabetes could be reversed in an extreme case such as mine. I had assumed that in my case, my diabetes could not be reversed nor cured.

What causes type 2 diabetes

Type 2 diabetes is caused when the body becomes insulin resistant. What this means is that, as we eat refined sugar in foods, over the years the sugar buildup overwhelms the body. The patient's pancreas still works; however, the insulin secreted by the pancreas is not able to transport all the excess sugar buildup into the cells to be used as energy to fuel the muscles. The sugar converts into fat which finds its way into the blood stream where it coats the cells. Once this happens, the cells are not able to absorb the sugar and transport it to other parts of our body, particularly, our muscles to be used as energy.

This is the point where the person loses energy and becomes insulin resistant—in other words, a type 2 diabetic.

Why is diabetes on the increase?

There are several factors to consider; for example, as the amount of processed foods and sweet drinks ingested increase, so does diabetes, according to researchers.

Additionally, diabetes is on the increase because of a lack of diabetes education which would provide diabetics with the correct information to help them heal.

How diabetes can be reversed

The solution is rather simple. If a diabetic body is insulin resistant, then to reverse the diabetes, the body's insulin sensitivity has to be restored.

Insulin sensitivity allows the sugar buildup to be used up, after which the body has no source of fuel but to burn fat for energy. This allows the fat that is in the blood stream and coating the cells to be burned, allowing the cells to function normally; thus, using the sugar for energy.

When the body has restored its insulin sensitivity, the diabetes is reversed.

How type 2 diabetes can be cured

"Cure" is a medical term that can trigger debate. This book was never intended to offer any form of medical advice or offer diagnoses or treatment for any sickness or disease. It was compiled for informational purposes.

For type 2 diabetes to be cured after it is reversed, the individual must not go back to the same lifestyle that caused the condition in the first place. If a physician saves the life of a patient with lung cancer caused by smoking, but the cured person returns to smoking, the lung cancer may come back.

There is overwhelming and mounting evidence that type 2 diabetes can be reversed, but most type 2 diabetics still don't know that their condition is reversible.

Type 2 diabetes is best reversed by:

1. following a personalized or customized menu cycle—not just by making meals randomly out of recipe books for diabetics

2. following a well-created, personalized exercise routine. But not just that—the routine should include the best time for the exercise to be executed, for how long, and what needs to happen during the exercise to let the person know that he or she is performing the exercise the way it was designed to be done

3. following a vitamin therapy and taking the vitamins at the right time of day.

What you are looking at is one sample of the meals which I used my background as a chef to create which helped me reverse my diabetes.

One of the meals I created which helped me reverse my diabetes.

The food has to be appealing and tasty for the diabetic to want to eat it. Many type 2 diabetics fail to reverse their condition, in most part, because they don't like the recipes they find in cook books for diabetics, most of which are written by chefs for the individual compiling the book. Often both the compiler and the chef do not have any idea about diabetes, let alone know how it feels like to struggle with it.

Here is my customized exercise routine. Within a month of starting this regimen, my energy level began to surge. In less than 30 days, Dr. Anthony Robinson declared me diabetes-free.

Day One	
Back	
Pulldown Front	15-reps - 25 reps - 25 reps
Seated rolls	15-reps - 15 reps - 15 reps
Close grip pulldown to front	15-reps - 15 reps - 15 reps
Legs	
Leg curl	15-reps - 15 reps - 15 reps
Leg extension	15-reps - 15 reps - 15 reps
Seated calf raise	15-reps - 15 reps - 15 reps
Inner thigh press	25-reps - 25 reps - 25 reps
25 minutes cardio on elliptical machine	

My customized exercise routine.

Even in my extreme case, I regained my health. What you are looking at is the test result from when my doctor pronounced me diabetes-free.

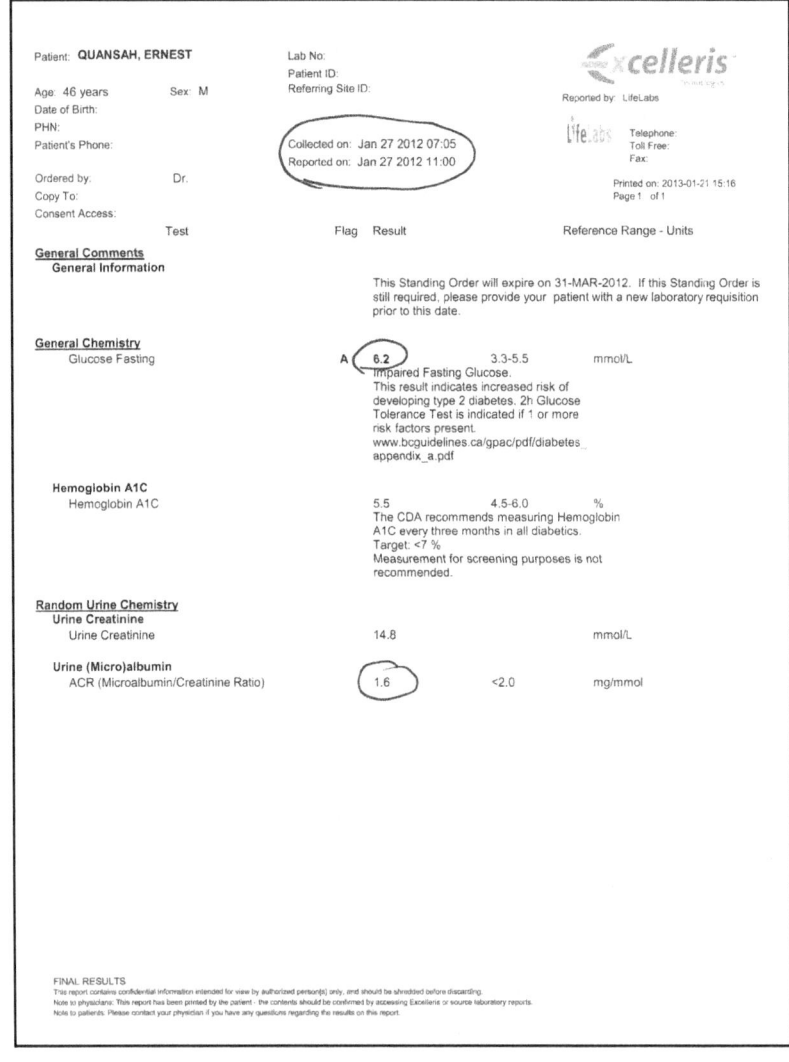

The test result from when my doctor pronounced me diabetes-free.

The purpose of my research was not just to help *me*; it was to help other type 2 diabetics reverse their type 2 diabetes.

Once my research had been completed and the diabetes was reversed, I had a discussion with Dr. Anthony Robinson about using the research results to help other diabetics. He replied, "That is an excellent idea." And he issued me a hand written testimonial to use in this book, which you have already seen in a previous chapter.

The efficacy of my research and system for helping heal diabetes was reviewed by Brunilda Nazario, MD, *WebMD* Lead Medical Editor and was featured in the magazine *WebMD Diabetes*, fall 2016 issue, page 19. The article can be found on their website.

WebMD, made up of hundreds of physicians, provides health care information to other medical doctors as well as the general public, such as diabetics.

The section of *WebMD* that the article appeared in is called "upClose." The first page of the article was given the following heading and subheading "My Secret Recipe: A chef shares his secrets for reversing type 2 diabetes." The second page has the heading and subheading "Secret Recipe: How a Chef Cured His Type 2 Diabetes." This article, based on an interview I had with *WebMD*, gives a summation of my journey, from being diagnosed with type 2 diabetes, to reversal of my condition, and finally, the cure. A few of my general tips on healthy living are given at the end. I was very pleased that such a well-renowned internet resource for medical information chose to make my story public and help spread the word that type 2 diabetes can certainly be reversed and cured.

Here is the URL to the article: http://www.webmd.com/diabetes/features/secret-recipe-how-a-chef-cured-his-type-2-diabetes#1

Other Research that Supports My Research Methodology

Back in 2012 when I began my research and discovered that sugar caused my type 2 diabetes, many in the healthcare profession said that type 2 diabetes was not caused by sugar. I am not alone in my assertion to the contrary. Earlier, I mentioned Dr. Robert Lustic, an American pediatric endocrinologist who is Professor of Pediatrics in the Division of Endocrinology at the University of California. His research links excess consumption of fructose (a constituent of refined sugar) with metabolic syndrome, which can include type 2 diabetes, high blood pressure, and other ailments.

Dr. Sanjay Basu, MSc, MD, Ph.D., an epidemiologist and Assistant Professor of Medicine at Stanford University has also linked sugar consumption to type 2 diabetes. An article published in *The Guardian* on February 27, 2013 entitled "Sugar is behind the global explosion in type 2 diabetes, study finds" reports on the research of Dr. Basu and his team of researchers. The opening thesis given in the article states Basu's finding that "sugar is behind the global explosion in type 2 diabetes."

Here is the URL to the article: https://www.theguardian.com/society/2013/feb/27/sugar-obesity-type-2-diabetes

As I said, I developed my methodology for reversing type 2 diabetes back in 2012. Research studies are now being conducted which are following suit with evidence that reversal and cure are indeed possible. The article, titled "Type 2 diabetes can be cured in four months—if you cut calories and exercise, research shows" was published on the *National Post* website on March 16, 2017. The same research study findings were published in the *Journal of Clinical Endocrinology & Metabolism*. I will give a brief summary of the findings given in the article.

The article begins by giving the results of a trial that was conducted on type 2 diabetics. The participants were given a personalized exercise program. This was coupled with a reduction in their daily calorie intake by 500 to 750. The participants continued to take their medications. Employing the two basic methods of a personalized exercise program and dieting, after four months, 40% of the participants no longer needed their medications because their bodies were again producing their own insulin. Dr. Natalia McInnes of McMaster University, Ontario, Canada, was quoted saying: "The research might shift the paradigm of treating diabetes from simply controlling glucose to an approach where we induce remission and then monitor patients for any signs of relapse."

As you can see from these findings and the conclusion of Dr. McInnes, my claim is strongly supported: Millions of type 2 diabetics around the world have an excellent chance of reversing their diabetes. My case was not really an exceptional occurrence and all type 2 diabetics should know this so they can be encouraged to take steps away from management toward a cure.

The article further paints the picture of the hugely growing number of cases of type 2 diabetes, citing the UK as an example. In financial terms, it talks about the Department of Health's cost in dealing with the condition and the great decrease in spending that would occur if a possible one million sufferers through the UK would be cured using the intervention methods just described. And yes my friends, they did use the word "cured."

Again, here is the URL: http://www.nationalpost.com/m/wp/health/blog.html?b=news.nationalpost.com/health/type-2-diabetes-can-be-cured-in-four-months-if-you-cut-calories-and-exercise-research-shows

⋆⋆⋆

In summation: I have related the story of my journey, which began with bad lifestyle choices, followed by being diagnosed with type 2 diabetes and then the life challenges I faced while dealing with my condition. I described how these circumstances propelled me toward my destiny—to do research, experiment on myself, and ultimately reverse and cure myself of my condition. I was blessed with the direction and guidance of my doctor and several other health practitioners. I have told you my story and shown you all the evidence of the success of my research and experimentation. I have included my blood test results and the hand-written testimonial of my doctor confirming this success. I sincerely hope that my findings and example can help diabetics all over the world overcome their type 2 diabetes and not just give into it.

My website offers the complete 3-Step Diabetes Reversal Program. All the specific details of the three factors (diet/menus, exercise, vitamins and supplements) are available in a single package of three separate manuals.

These manuals are available for a very small charge. It is up to you if you want to take up the challenge and show the determination to achieve your own results. All the tools are there for you.

My very best wishes,
Ernest

WEBSITE: https://diabeticsjourney.com
DIABETES CURE WEBSITE: https://discoverdiabetesselfcure.com
Copyright 2017 Discover Diabetes Self-Cure. All rights reserved.
Discover Diabetes Self-Cure does not provide medical advice, diagnosis, or treatment.

About the Author

ERNEST QUANSAH, BORN in Ghana, West Africa, moved to Canada in 1982. He is an avid reader, especially of books related to psychology, health and fitness. In 2009, he was diagnosed a type 2 diabetic. After managing the diabetes, he decided to become a diabetes researcher. This undertaking led to the discovery of a three-step program; diet, exercise, and vitamin therapy, which reversed his diabetes. His diabetes-reversal methodology was so effective that it was reviewed by *WebMD*'s lead medical editor and featured in the *WebMD Diabetes* fall 2016 issue, page 19.

Visit Quansah's website to learn about the 3-Step Type 2 Diabetes Self-Cure Program that reverses and cures type 2 diabetes.

Other Books by Ernest Quansah

How to Identify Your Soulmate: A Comprehensive Guide Book for Finding Your Soulmate

A number of years ago, "soulmates" was a hot topic. At that time, Ernest performed his own study on what makes two people soulmates; the joy such a relationship brings; the emotional and intuitive connection of the couple; and the healing power of a soulmate relationship. He felt that people should be privy to the information he found and so he wrote *How to Identify Your Soulmate*. People who bought the manual commented that it was very accurate and helped them know who their soulmate was.

Rating: This book received a 4-star rating.

How to Identify Your Soulmate
ISBN-13: 978-146-638-526-9
You can order by visiting https://ernestquansah.com

Dos and Don'ts of Relationships: Nine Steps to a Deeper, Richer Love Relationship

After researching about soulmates and eventually experiencing such a relationship first hand, Ernest's interest in Relationship Counselling grew. He wanted to contribute something to help singles find true love and couples strengthen their love relationships. He enrolled in a philosophical counselling program. At that time, a degree program could only be obtained in European universities. Ernest settled for Peer Counselling, a one-year counselling certificate program at the University of British Columbia. Upon completion of the certificate program, he embarked on counselling online in addition to doing research and administering a survey related to his research in which he learned that everyone, despite relationship failures and divorce rates, said that they believed in love and happiness and would like to find true love, if someone could show them how. The responses to the survey, as well as Ernest's counselling experience, led to the compilation of *Dos and Don'ts of Relationships*. This book has something for everyone. Ernest has successfully assisted singles to find a suitable partner and fall in love. Some who found partners are still married, 10 years on. This successful work is a one-stop love and relationship book covering these topics:

- how and where to find a date
- the three categories of relationships and where yours fit in
- the answer to whether women are smarter than men

- conflict resolution techniques in relationship
- why women change their minds
- why men cheat
- how to make your significant other love you so much that he or she never cheats on you
- avoiding toxic relationship
- healing from an abusive relationship
- techniques for fixing deficiencies and making a marriage blossom
- how to create an exit strategy if it is the only option left
- much more.

Rating: It has received an average 4.5-star rating and has been referred to as groundbreaking—a great success for his second book.

Dos and Don'ts of Relationships
ISBN: 13: 978-1-46643-316-8
You can order by visiting https://ernestquansah.com

Seniors' Emotional Care: A Baby Boomer's Guide to Caring for Mom or Dad

While Ernest was working as a manager in residential care facilities, he learned firsthand what the residents wanted besides good, tasty food, emotional care, and emotional support. His research into the matter led him to interview Dr. Andrew Sixsmith, Ph.D.,

Director of Gerontology at Simon Fraser University. At the end of his research, he authored *Seniors' Emotional Care*, endorsed by Dr. Sixsmith. *Seniors' Emotional Care* was written to guide people with elderly parents in care by showing them how alleviate their parents' feelings of loneliness, abandonment, and isolation, all of which are common causes of depression.

Seniors' Emotional Care
ISBN-13: 978-1496195722
You can order by visiting https://ernestquansah.com

www.ingramcontent.com/pod-product-compliance
Lightning Source LLC
Chambersburg PA
CBHW070622300426
44113CB00010B/1625